T0204711

THE STORY OF A SOLDIER AND A PHARAOH

A JOURNEY
BETWEEN SOULS

ELAINE EDGAR

edited by
Colin White & Lorraine McWilliams

WHITE
BOUCKE
PUBLISHING

LAFAYETTE, COLORADO

ISBN: 1-888580-00-3
Library of Congress Catalog Card Number: 96-61841
Printed in USA

WHITE BOUCKE
PUBLISHING
PO BOX 400 LAFAYETTE CO 80026 USA

To the Edgar family:
to Royce for his endless
support and encouragement;
to my sons Simon and Cliff,
and my daughters Sarah and Lisa
for their patience and understanding.

* * * * * * * *

A Journey Between Souls could not have been completed without the valuable advice, assistance and contributions made by the following:

Aramco World (John Lawton, Tor Eigeland and Robert Arndt)
Jean Armstrong (Millom Library)
Anthony Bales (Bales Tours Ltd.)
Suzanne Bojtos (Petrie Museum of Egyptian Archaeology)
British Museum (W.V. Davies, John Hayman, A.J. Spencer
and John H. Taylor)
Mr. Buxton (Purbrook Junior School Hampshire)
The Rt. Hon. The Earl of Carnarvon, KCVO, KBE, DL
Mrs. J. Thorpe (Archivist to the Highclere Estate)
Mrs. N. Sutcliffe (Secretary to the Earl of Carnarvon)
Rosemary Deignan (Camden Graphics Ltd.)
Joe D. Henry (Cumbria Heritage Services)
Dennis Hollands City of Rochester upon Medway
Cathy Halton (Tyne-Tees Television)
Mavis Hayward ("mum")
Caroline James
Mary Lally (Richard's "Sister Lally")
Geraldine Lancaster
Jayne Logan (H.T.V. Wales)
Donald Martin (Editor, North West Evening Mail)
Beryl McAllister (Copeland Borough Council)
Dr. Jaromir Malek and Sue Hutchison
(Griffith Institute Ashmolean Museum, Oxford)
Zoe Mayne (Transworld Publishers Ltd.)
Roger Murray
Tricia, Phil and Greg North
Mrs. L. O'Rourke (The Royal Star & Garter Home)
The Palladium Committee, Millom Cumbria
Allan Percival (Press Secretary to H.R.H. The Prince of Wales)

Lee & Pembertons and The Executors of Mervyn Herbert
Diana Ring (St. Antony's College, Oxford)
Neville Robson (Robson's Photos)
Sandra Sljivic
Geoffrey Skelsey (University of Cambridge)
Ron and Jill Slaughter
Janice Savage
Patricia Spencer (Secretary, Egypt Exploration Society)
Lt. Col. Squier (Curator, Royal Military Police Museum)
Olwen Terris (British Film Institute)
The News, Portsmouth
Babs Warren
Edward Workman

* * * * * * * *

Special thanks to . . .
Mohamed Gamal el din Montisir,
for sharing his beloved country with me.

Colin and Laurie at White-Boucke Publishing, without
their help and involvement, this project would
probably have crash landed.

Finally, for untiring attention, efforts and
understanding, thanks to Kevin, David and John
Adamson and their respective families.
I hope I have done justice to your grandfather.

* * * * * * * *

CONTENTS

PHOTO AND ILLUSTRATION CREDITS

Page	Caption	Credit
i	*(phonograph)*	Bradley Keough
2	The Duke of Wellington's...	unknown
2	Richard Adamson	unknown
3	The "Escort Party" to...	unknown
5	A Cairo bazaar...	unknown
7	Ceremonial dagger accession...	Royal Military Police Mus.
14	*(map)*	Colin White
16	A mud brick village...	Elaine Edgar
17	The Winter Palace Hotel...	Ron Slaughter
24	Statue of Pharaoh Tutankhamun...	P. North
26	*(map)*	Colin White
28	"Castle Carter"...	Elaine Edgar
35	The ruins of workmen's huts...	Griffith Institute
36	Foundations above the tomb...	Griffith Institute
40	The entrance to the tomb...	P. North
41	The Valley of the Kings...	Griffith Institute
49	*(telegrams)*	---
50/51	Mace, Callender, Lady Evelyn...	Times Newspapers Ltd.

FOREWORD

Many books have been written on the 1922 discovery of the tomb of Pharaoh Tutankhamun. The earliest tomes typically were authored by members of the discovery expedition, while later books have presented a variety of hypotheses on the myriad of mysteries concerning the pharaoh, the principal discoverers and the current-day status of the tomb's treasures.

Almost all of these works have a common denominator: the absence of any reference to a British military policeman who arrived in the Valley of the Kings but a day before the find, was a central character in the unearthing of the first few steps, and was the only man to remain on-site with Howard Carter until 1932 when the tomb was completely cleared.

Acting Sergeant Richard Adamson is not even identified by Howard Carter himself in his famous three-volume written work on the subject, *The Tomb of Tut-ankh-Amen.* Carter does, however, make at least two veiled references to the soldier in relation to tomb security. The first is in Volume 1, Chapter 5, where Carter describes events following the uncovering of a sealed door at the foot of the entrance stairwell:

> ". . . I re-closed the small hole that I had made, filled in our evacuation for protection during the night, selected the most trustworthy of my workmen to watch all night above the tomb . . . "

The second reference is in Volume 1, Chapter 8, where Carter addresses the arrangements made to protect the recently discovered treasures:

> ". . . we had a heavy wooden grille at the entrance to the passageway, and a massive steel gate at the inner doorway, each secured by four padlocked chains; and, that there might never be any mistake about these latter, the keys were in the permanent charge of one particular member of the European staff, who never parted with them for a moment . . ."

So why the mystery? The simple answer is that Adamson, an ordinary soldier, was posted to the valley to protect him from death threats issued by the extremist and powerful Wafd Party in Cairo. He needed "invisibility"—and that is exactly what he got from Carter and the other expedition members. In fact, he remained anonymous for nearly half a century until, as the last surviving member of the discovery expedition, he toured and lectured around Great Britain for the remaining years of his life.

Some critics of Richard Adamson's story eagerly indicate that the extensive photographic record of the discovery of Tutankhamun's tomb contains no evidence of his involvement. Although this is true, the photographs cited are mostly catalogue items recording tomb objects, locations, etc. The remainder are, in effect, carefully choreographed and posed portraits of the principal players, on-site academics, visiting dignitaries and officials. There was no reason to include a lowly soldier who was "in hiding" at the time.

Although Adamson was originally unhappy with his posting to the Valley of the Kings and not always enamoured of Howard Carter, he gained much respect and admiration for the tireless and meticulous archaeologist to the point of steadfastly defending Carter's honour at all times. There have been repeated allegations that Carter and others explored the tomb's chambers earlier than officially reported, and that Carter perhaps removed a few small objects for himself. Adamson firmly refused to give credence to such claims, but there remains the possibility that Adamson was not privy to all the events that transpired in the Valley of the Kings.

A Journey Between Souls is the only biography of Richard Adamson. Author Elaine Edgar first met him in the mid-1970s and was a close friend and confidante until his death in 1982. The material presented in this book is, for the most part, sourced from Adamson himself and his surviving family. The Adamson "diary entries" that appear in the earlier chapters are author-reconstructions of Richard Adamson's thoughts, feelings and observations, based on Mrs. Edgar's many discussions with Adamson. The content and style of these entries have been confirmed as "typical" and described as "credible" by members of Adamson's immediate family.

Colin White,
Publisher.

1

ORDERS

CORPORAL R. ADAMSON PROMOTED TO RANK
OF ACTING SERGEANT. PROCEED IMMEDIATELY
TO LUXOR AND REPORT TO MR. HOWARD
CARTER, C/O LORD CARNARVON'S EXPEDITION,
WINTER PALACE HOTEL.

October 1922. A British military policeman stepped down onto the platform at Luxor railway station, weary after the 450-mile haul from Cairo. He slowly pushed his way through the throng and out into the hazy night air, aware that his tall, uniformed body and red cap band made him more than conspicuous. He made his way out of the station and asked directions to the Winter Palace Hotel, determined to make the best of his "orders" and wondering what was in store.

Richard Leslie Adamson was born on 10 January 1901, in Yorkshire, England, the son of a wholesale tailor from the industrial town of Leeds. He saw action in France during World War I as an infantryman in the Duke of Wellington's

photographer unknown

The Duke of Wellington's Regiment

Richard Adamson

photographer unknown

Regiment (now the Middlesex Regiment) before being transferred to the military police. He possessed the attitude and outspokenness of the northern working man, a manner but mildly restrained after years of military service.

His easy-going nature manifested itself on the battlefields of France. When instructed to walk around a dead body that lay slumped against the sandbags in an occupied trench, Richard climbed up onto the parapet to avoid the corpse. In so doing, he narrowly escaped being blown to pieces and later admitted to not even knowing how to fire his rifle properly.

Following the end of hostilities in 1918, his regiment travelled to Gibraltar and three weeks later boarded a troopship bound for the Turkish city of Constantinople (now Istanbul). Although stationed in Turkey for only three weeks, he was part of the squad of five soldiers who arrested Mustafa Kemal (later Kemal Ataturk, President of Turkey), the

photographer unknown

"Escort Party" to Mustafa Kemal, Bostandjik, Turkey, 1919 (Richard Adamson front centre)

man responsible for the defeat of the Allied Forces at Gallipoli in 1915.

Political unrest in the Egyptian capital of Cairo in 1919 created the necessity for action once again. "Volunteers" were urgently needed to boost the ranks of the military police in Cairo. Richard became one such volunteer, one of the many souls almost press-ganged into sharing the ordeals under the requirements of the military police, whether he liked it or not.

"How long would I be required?" he asked in a typically outright manner. The answer: "Permanent."

He signed up for duty, was promoted to full corporal and once again received orders to embark—this time for Cairo via the north-eastern Egyptian city of Port Said.

He arrived at the Bab-el-Hadid barracks in Cairo around noon. It was a somewhat gruff Yorkshireman that marched out of the barracks two hours later on a lone patrol through the unfamiliar streets of the city. The only briefing he was given was to "walk in the middle of the road to avoid trouble and report to the patrol point at 1600 hours."

Several hours later (although it felt like days to Richard), a search party found the new recruit, who was already less than enamoured with his role as a military policeman in Egypt's capital. The following day Richard asked his colleagues if anybody had ever "got lost" before.

"One or two," came a sarcastic reply.

"What happened to them?"

"Never been seen again."

This seemed to cure Richard of his wanderings.

artist unknown

A Cairo bazaar in the early 1900s

Oh, those Friday nights in Cairo! At 2130 hours, the British and Indian troops received their pay. The combined forces of the military police foot and mounted patrols entered the brothel areas. Their mission: to unearth those who had gone to ground and to separate the men from the boys. The scene was of carnage as bottles, knives and missiles of all kinds were hurled, and abuse pitched around on all sides before any semblance of order was regained.

Despite experiencing the horrors of World War I, Richard's mind was indelibly stamped with the image of the "blood wagons"—carts filled with drunken, bleeding prisoners being transferred to the military and civil gaols— and lines of mounted police strung out across the street, with unmentionable acts being perpetrated to bring the rowdies to heel. Richard hated his involvement in these engagements and would later relay the details with ultimate disgust.

Fortunately, some of his duties were of a more peaceful nature. One in particular was when he was checking credentials on the Kantara side of a wooden bridge spanning the Suez Canal. A party of 12 men approached and their leader, an impressive gentleman sporting a large black hat and a long beard, proffered his pass. He confirmed that their destination was Palestine. After glancing at the papers, Richard looked at the leader of the group and said, "Yes, sir, these seem to be in order. You may pass."

The man replied quietly, "We have been waiting 2,000 years to hear those words."

"What do you mean?" Richard enquired.

"Never mind," came the reply.

Shortly after, Richard turned to the Egyptian policeman beside him and asked, "Who was that then?"

"Dr. Weizmann—the Jewish leader."

He was temporarily transferred to Palestine (now Israel) to enhance the British military police presence in Jerusalem. At the time, martial law had been proclaimed and a curfew imposed during the gentile Feast of the Holy Fire, which was being observed at the time of the Jewish Feast of the Passover. Richard's mission was to guard the Jaffa Gate in Old Jerusalem—everyone passing through the Gate had to be searched. Ugly scenes sometimes occurred when Muslim taboos regarding womenfolk were necessarily violated. Of all the weapons discovered, three-quarters were found upon women. Perhaps the most vicious of the weapons Richard confiscated was a razor-sharp serrated dagger, which is currently housed in the Royal Military Police Museum, Chichester.

MISC.

ACCN NO: .1040... CLASSIFICATION: .WEAPONS.. DATE:/2/5/6.4.

DESCRIPTION   Ceremonial dagger Jerusalem 1920

DONATED BY: Mr R Adamson (Ex Sgt)

ALSO DONATED: LOCATION : Cupboard
1.   Goodwood
2.   ....HSM (XI/90)
3.
4.

REMARKS
Arab dagger taken from a Arab woman
by Sgt. Adamson during Jerusalem Riots

Royal Military Police Museum

*Royal Military Police Museum accession
document for the "ceremonial dagger"
confiscated by Adamson in Jerusalem*

As Richard noted in a report on the incident:

> ". . . It was asking for trouble that these
> religious observances should take place at the same
> time, and trouble is what we got . . ."

He was very angry because he felt tragedy could easily
have been avoided. On the second night of the curfew, an
Indian policeman shot and killed an elderly Arab woman
who was apparently unaware of the curfew. Demonstrations
followed, and an attempt was made to capture the Jaffa
Gate:

> ". . . I gave orders to fire above the heads of the
> mob. This dispersed the first attack, but several
> more were made during the day and night, each
> dispersed by revolver fire.
>
> The following day, I was told that a large mob
> had assembled outside the Holy Sepulchre and that

the Patriarch feared an attempt upon it, and sought my help. Although I had an armoured car, the packed streets prevented me from reaching headquarters, which could not be contacted because telephone wires had been torn down. I had to leave my car at the Jaffa Gate . . ."

Taking some Indian policemen with him, he proceeded to the Holy Sepulchre where the patriarch was indeed very glad to see him, as some of the mob had forced its way into the building during the service. The patriarch went to the aid of a fallen policeman. At this point, a demonstrator moved forward to attack the priest. Richard, having witnessed this development, took action:

". . . I fired at him, wounding him, and then fired again over the heads of the crowd. They drew back a little and after we had advanced, revolvers in hand, we succeeded in getting them outside and I closed the doors.

Later the crowds dispersed, but I remained at the Holy Sepulchre for the rest of the day and night, sleeping inside, one of the few Englishmen, I believe, ever to have done so."

Richard Adamson was not a man with religious convictions, but throughout his life he respected the beliefs of others—no matter how obscure. His reverence to the rites and rituals of the Jewish faith, while honouring those of others, was certainly a factor in defusing the situation. This was the first time that a shrine in Jerusalem had been attacked since the days of King Solomon, and it had been defended by a member of the British military police.

An official report on the riots was forwarded to Lord Allenby, the senior British military official in the region, but it made no mention of the attack on the Holy Sepulchre.

Allenby had previously given instructions that religious services of different denominations should not take place concurrently. Richard later recalled, "When I met Lord Allenby, it was at the time of the discovery of the tomb of Tutankhamun—he was by then the High Commissioner for Egypt. I found out that he had never been told of the attack upon the Holy Sepulchre. He was a great and wise soldier and statesman, and would have solved this situation, had he been kept informed." If formal measures had been taken then to settle the differences between Arab and Jew, later troubles might not have come about. Instead, martial law prevailed, leaving the bitter hatred of centuries still smoldering.

On his return to Cairo, Richard transferred to the military police "staff" at the British Embassy, which was to be his posting on and off for the next three years.

Life improved for Richard. His duties at the Embassy were far less hazardous than his prior experiences in the Middle East. He remembered seeing Lord Carnarvon at the Embassy quite frequently, but had never uttered more than a polite, "Good morning, my Lord." Howard Carter had apparently also been a regular visitor, although Richard did not remember seeing him.

Egypt's desire to shed the last remains of British colonial rule was growing. There were increasing hostilities and demonstrations in the streets. One such incident involved a young Egyptian student, Hassenein Ali, a member of the nationalist Wafd (or "delegation") Party. He had hurled a hand grenade at the Egyptian Prime Minister, believing him to be Sir Lee Stack, the Governor of the Sudan. It was an abortive attempt, and the student was captured, convicted and later hanged for the crime.

Richard had escorted the young Egyptian throughout the trial and was therefore detailed to attend the execution. Due to circumstances resulting from that, Richard was able to gain information which ultimately led to the Cairo Police Chief issuing arrest warrants for leading members of the Wafd Party. Richard's own notes regarding the matter read like a formal statement and give much insight into the events of the day:

THE CAIRO CONSPIRACY TRIAL
(by Richard Adamson)

The Cairo Conspiracy Trial began in 1920 with the arraignment of a leader of the Wafd Party— Abdul Rhaman Fahy Bey[1] [*sic*] and 28 other prisoners before a British military court charged with conspiring to overthrow British rule in Egypt. How did this come about? A few weeks before this trial, an Egyptian student, Hassenein Ali, had been tried by a military court of attempting to kill the Egyptian Prime Minister Nessim Pasha[2] by throwing a bomb at him. He was found guilty, sentenced to death and duly executed.

The outcome of this was that eventually I did get into conversation with Rhaman, and I told him what the student Hassenein Ali had said with reference to Sir Lee Stack. Abdul Rhaman replied that he had paid the price for "his mistake." During the trial, I had to accompany the president of the court, General Lawson, to and from his hotel (the Continental) and wherever he went at other times.

---

1. Abdul Rahman Fahmi, then Secretary of the Wafdist Central Committee.
2. Tawfiq Nessim, twice Prime Minister of Egypt.

One morning on our way to the court, we encountered a huge procession parading the streets to welcome back the peace delegate from London.

The demonstration was anti-British and as the car in which we were travelling was outlying a Union Jack from the bonnet, I suggested to the General, who also had the Judge Advocate-General with him, that we should go round by some side streets. General Lawson said no, but to go the same way, as everyone knew who was in this car. I thought it advisable to be ready for any eventuality and withdrew my revolver from its holster and laid it on my lap.

We had an Arab driver whom I did not at all trust (despite my objections, he had not been replaced) and as we proceeded slowly through the crowd near the Shepherd's Hotel, the car knocked down a small Arab girl. The General told me not to leave the car and instructed the driver to find out if the girl was badly injured. The driver got out and disappeared in the crowd which gathered round threateningly. Acting upon a sudden impulse, I took the wheel and told an Egyptian girl to pick up the child and get in the car. The girl picked up the child and got into the car next to me. I shouted, "I'm going to the hospital," and the crowd immediately gave way.

The General told me to take the child to the hospital first. We then proceeded to the court without further incident. The child was not badly hurt.

During the trial I, as a member of the military police, acted as his [Hassenein Ali] escort and had to remain with the prisoner throughout the trial. In the dock he confided in me a great deal and informed me that he had acted under the orders of the Wafd (Nationalist) party and the intention had been to kill the Sirdar of the Egyptian army and the Governor of the Sudan, Sir Lee Stack, but a mistake had been made resulting in an attack upon the Prime Minister instead.

I passed this information to General Lawson. The outcome of this was an investigation by the Commandant of the Cairo police, Russell Pasha,[3] and the eventual arrest of members of the Wafd Party. The Judge Advocate-General of the military court was Mr. Linton-Thorpe K.C. (later Chairman of the Middlesex Assizes) and Abdul Rhaman engaged Mr. Mitchel Innes K.C. as his leading counsel at an enormous fee.

During the trial, I acted as a personal escort to the president of the court, General Lawson. At first, following a threat to kill the General, I sat next to him on the bench, from which position I could see the whole court. Later the General requested me to sit in the dock with the other police and try to get into conversation with Abdul Rhaman.

The prisoners were all found guilty of attempting to overthrow British rule in Egypt. Abdul Rhaman Fahy Bey and four others were sentenced to death and the remainder to long terms of imprisonment. The death sentences were, however, never carried out and substituted to life imprisonment for fear of open revolt. I asked General Lawson what action should be taken regarding the threat to Sir Lee Stack, but he would

---

3. Thomas Russell, who at this time was officially "assistant" to Commandant Harvey in Cairo. He later became Inspector General of Egyptian Police.

not take it seriously, and I therefore approached Russell Pasha. He also contacted General Lawson. Russell was for further investigation but was overruled by the General.

I was told to write a letter explaining all the facts to the Foreign Secretary in London, and was eventually interviewed by officials of the Foreign Office to whom I gave details of my conversations with Hassenein Ali.

Precautions were taken and Sir Lee Stack advised of what had transpired. Unfortunately, the next attempt succeeded and he was assassinated in Cairo.

The revoking of the death sentences of those prisoners who had been sentenced to death proved to be a mistake. The Wafd Party became stronger and planted the seeds that eventually bore fruit in the final overthrow of the treaty some years later.

What would have been the outcome had we taken a strong line at the time can only be surmised, but it is a fact that respect for Britain began to dwindle from that time, and British influence took the downward step. It is open to conjecture if the assassination of Sir Lee Stack would have taken place had the death sentences been carried out on the members of the Wafd Party.

The British protectorate could have continued beyond 1922, and Sultan Ahmed Fuad would have never been proclaimed king, which paved the way for the overthrow of the Government by Mohammed Neguib Pasha and all that followed leading up to the Suez affair and to British rule and influence in Egypt coming to an end forever.

The aftermath of this historic trial made life very dangerous for Adamson. It was a very precarious business— so much so that it was tactfully insisted that "Cpl. Adamson get posted away from Cairo as soon as possible, for his own safety." A few days later fresh orders arrived, and soon he was on his way to Luxor . . . and the Valley of the Kings.

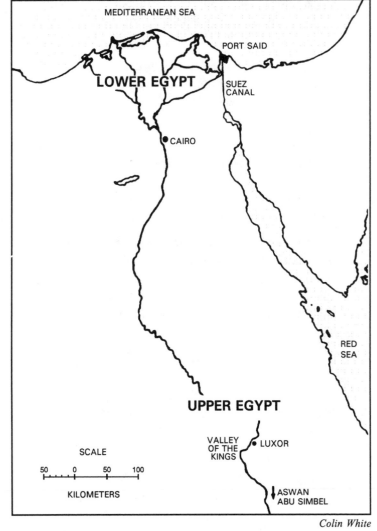

Colin White

* * * * * * * *

2

WHAT, ME SIR?

31 October 1922. The long train journey from Cairo to Luxor seems endless. My uniform is sticking to my body like glue in this airless carriage. Even for October I have to expect 10 degrees hotter in Luxor and although I am well used to the heat, I shall indeed be glad to reach my destination today.

As I look out at the odd palm grove and the mud-brick villages as the train rattles by them, it all seems more peaceful than the hectic pace of Cairo. Perhaps I will get a chance to see something of the place for the short time I have here. I must try to fit in a visit to the temples before I leave. They are all probably covered in sand, judging by the amount that is visible from where I am sitting. It's desolate and unrelenting terrain by the seem of things. I'd hate to be alone out there, the Bedouin are welcome to it all . . .

Elaine Edgar

*A mud brick village between
Cairo and Luxor, 1991*

The Winter Palace Hotel, Luxor, is a large impressive building overlooking the Nile. As Richard walked up the grand stairway and into the foyer of the hotel that evening in October 1922, he recalled that it was rather like walking into a time warp. The lavish interior contrasted dramatically with what he had seen of Egypt thus far. However, the cushioned comfort of luxury accommodation was not to be had by a mere soldier in exile. His room was small, basic but clean, and located in the inelegant rear of the building. He accepted that some things never change, feeling it was enough that he had quarters for the night.

He freshened up, then went down to the hotel bar hoping to contact Lord Carnarvon or Mr. Carter and report for duty. The hotel manager told him it would be unlikely that either would be available that evening. Not deterred,

Richard approached a distinguished-looking gentleman sitting alone in the lounge and, after making polite conversation, discovered he was speaking with the Hon. Mervyn Herbert, half-brother to Lord Carnarvon. This short talk led to an introduction to His Lordship, who seemed surprised that the soldier had arrived so soon. Richard was asked whether he had eaten and, once the usual courtesies had been observed, was told to report to Carter first thing next morning.

Ron Slaughter

The Winter Palace Hotel, Luxor

Having now been "dismissed," Richard decided to take a stroll in the moonlight before retiring for the night. He crossed the street to the eastern bank of the Nile and lingered awhile. The feluccas were harnessed and the night was still:

> *... Took a walk before turning in for the night.*
> *The hotel is right on the corniche so I only had to*
> *walk across the road to get to the river. Some horse-*

drawn carriages passed me as I walked, but I declined their offerings to take me on a sight-seeing tour of the town, I just wanted to breathe the night air into my lungs after the journey from Cairo. Almost tempted to sleep out under the stars tonight, like some of the locals appear to. Saw a couple of bundles of clothing wrapped up into heaps with their owners snoring loudly as I passed by them.

I noticed an old chap having a smoke and we struck up a conversation, his English being adequate for the task. He started to explain a little to me about the town, then got carried away at one point when he elaborated on a question I put to him about the Nile. A simple question, I thought, about how it seemed to provide the land either side of its banks with lush green crops. The old boy got excited at this point and we somehow got on to the ancient Egyptian god of the Nile—Hapi—and all the myths and legends came tumbling out.

Hapi had apparently lived in a cave in ancient times and just came out at the time of the annual flood: the season called inundation! There had been celebrations and sacrifice, and it all became confused in my mind, all this talk of beautiful young virgins being hurled into the flow just to satisfy the river-god. It seemed to be such a waste somehow; but still, it was all part and parcel of the need for the annual flood to be a "moderate" one—neither a torrent nor a drought, just a moderate flood that would leave a regular silt upon the land, enough to provide the population with crops, enough to get them through their hard toil for yet another year. I would have been inclined to just throw the odd roll of papyrus in the water with a wing and a prayer, and hope that would appease this Hapi chappy.

All I can say is, thank God the modern-day Egyptians who still celebrate the "Sacrifice of the Nile Flood" use a dummy instead of a tender young maiden.

I was intrigued by the old man's tales as he rambled on, then thought that he may expect some "baksheesh" for his trouble, but no ... he simply bade me good-night, having wished me a happy stay in Luxor.

Nice chap, I thought, and much better than the "welcome" I had received from the rather offhand hotel manager as I walked into the foyer earlier that day. Still, I must have looked a sorry sight when I come to think about it, tired, hungry, hot and sweaty, upsetting all those posh punters in their glad rags. I noticed how quickly I was ushered up to my room at the back. A bit basic too, but what can I expect? I am not an officer. So as long as I have quarters for the night ... When I think back, though, I have fought for King and country, so why shouldn't I expect a little sympathy when I arrive. No, I am getting too soft. I am a soldier. I just hope it's a soft bed tonight! ...

The next morning he was up at sunrise and had eaten a hearty breakfast by the time he was informed that Howard Carter would like to see him in the garden. Richard wandered into the garden which was empty except for a European couple sitting beneath some trees. It seemed obvious that here was his man. As he approached the bench, he enquired, "Mr. Carter, sir?"

"Yes, good morning."

"Sergeant Adamson, sir, from Cairo."

"Yes, very good to see you. Did you sleep well?"

19

"Indeed I did, sir, thank you."

At this point the young lady companion made her excuses and left the two men to their conversation.

"Sit down, Adamson."

"Thank you, sir. By the way, Mr. Carter, I saw Lord Carnarvon last night."

"Did you indeed. When was that then?" Carter seemed surprised.

"Last evening, sir, soon after I arrived."

"You were lucky then. He left for Cairo first thing this morning."

"Left, sir?"

"Yes, he left us this morning. He's finished with us now. He only came down for a day from Cairo to tidy up business. You were lucky to see him. I only had an hour with him myself. His interest in this excavation is over. We have virtually completed our task. He is en route to England. In fact, this was only a very short visit. He has been travelling in Greece."

Carter noticed a quizzical look on Richard's face and enquired, "Don't you know why you have been called down here?"

"No, sir, not really. We never know anything in the army until it is happening. I had to leave Cairo for my own safety, so here I am."

Howard Carter remarked to Richard that bureaucracy was the same the world over and went on to explain that Lord Carnarvon and he had been conducting a "dig" in the Valley of the Kings on the West Bank. They were almost finished and were packing up. The army had loaned the expedition some survey equipment and Richard's task was to inventory this equipment and then arrange for it to be shipped back to Cairo.

Richard was flabbergasted. "What, me sir?"

"Yes, you. Now, are you ready?"

"Sir, I cannot understand it. I thought I would be joining the staff of Lord Carnarvon."

Although not known to be a patient man, Carter again explained that the survey equipment was to be crated and shipped, and added that Sergeant Adamson would be returning to Cairo when this was done. Richard frantically explained to his new "commander" just why he had had to leave, and stay out of, Cairo. Even though the situation had been fully explained, it did nothing to solve the problem for Richard. He was only going to be in Luxor for a short while.

The two men made their way down to the ferry, each no doubt wondering what the next few days would decide.

* * * * * * * *

The early pharaohs tried hard to foil tomb robbers. Originally, burial sites consisted of underground tombs surmounted by rectangular brick superstructures. Each "mastaba" grave was accessed through a vertical shaft which was closed and sealed with rubble for protection. By the 3rd Dynasty, the mastaba had been replaced by the "stepped pyramid" which was effectively a series of mastaba super-structures built on top of another, the number of layers being indicative of the status of the deceased. Later, to add a degree of architectural style, the layers were disguised by filling in the steps to form perfect pyramids. The chamber(s) were moved to within the mounds and for added security, false passages were constructed, as were dummy chambers and secret doors. But the robbers overcame all these obstacles. By the beginning of the 18th Dynasty, there was hardly a pharaoh's tomb in Egypt that had not been stripped of its contents.

The pharaohs then decided to revert to the underground chamber concept and concentrate royal tombs within a restricted area where maximum security could be provided both by location and tomb design. Thirty kings of the 18th and 19th Dynasties, their wives, children and numerous other dignitaries were thus buried in desolate, steep-sided canyons on the west bank of the Nile, opposite the ancient city of Thebes (now Luxor): the Valley of the Kings, the Valley of the Queens and the Valley of the Nobles. For a time the royal tombs remained relatively secure, under the protection of a para-religious organisation called the Royal Necropolis. But by the 20th Dynasty, the cemetery guardians had became so lax and corrupt that widespread looting took place once again.

Centuries after the demise of the Ancient Egyptian culture, Italian explorer Giovanni Belzoni unearthed many individual tombs in the valley-cemeteries. Excavations in and around the tomb of Seti I started in 1819, and work has continued ever since. By the turn of the 20th century, over 60 tombs had been found in the Theban Hills. However, a gap in the chronology of the 18th Dynasty posed many questions in the minds of contemporary archaeologists.

Theodore M. Davis, a retired millionaire lawyer from Newport, Rhode Island, had visited Upper Egypt in the 1890s as an archaeology enthusiast looking for a suitable project and was more than a little impressed with what he saw in the Theban Hills. As a result, he financed the Egyptian Department of Antiquities to explore the valleys further. Howard Carter was working for Davis when the tombs of Pharaohs Tuthmosis and Siptah, and the elaborate funerary temple of Queen Hatshepsut, were discovered.

Carter had arrived in Egypt in 1891 when he was only 17 years old as the junior member of the Egypt Exploration Fund, a private organisation linked to the British Museum. His task as a water-colourist was to record the paintings, reliefs and inscriptions at various sites, including the temple of Queen Hatshepsut. Despite his lack of formal training, he quickly became an accomplished archaeologist and Egyptologist. In 1899 at age 25, for example, Carter was appointed Chief Inspector of Antiquities in Upper Egypt, with headquarters in Luxor.

Carter developed an archaeological passion to dig in the Valley of the Kings. He firmly believed that there were still significant discoveries to be made in that region. In particular, he was troubled by the lack of artifacts relating to the Pharaoh Tutankhamun, the 18th Dynasty boy-king who had reigned from approximately 1334 to 1323 B.C. Three finds reinforced his belief that the tomb was hidden somewhere in the valley. One was a blue-glazed cup bearing the cartouche of Tutankhamun, found beneath a rock. The second was a cache of large jars bearing evidence of the Pharaoh's funerary feast. The third was a small pit tomb containing pieces of gold foil bearing the name of Tutankhamun. Theodore Davis assumed the pit to be the remains of the Pharaoh's burial place, but Carter argued that it was "ludicrously inadequate" for a king's burial.

Carter's ambition to dig independently in the valley was realised through two completely unrelated events. The first was a feud between Howard Carter and the Department of

P. North

A remaining statue of the
Pharaoh Tutankhamun
at the temple of Karnak

Antiquities, which led to his resignation as Chief Inspector in 1905. The second was a car accident in Germany, which resulted in serious injury to the Rt. Hon. George Edward Stanhope Molyneux Herbert, fifth Earl of Carnarvon. After swerving to avoid a collision, Carnarvon was pinned beneath his car and nearly asphyxiated at the bottom of a soft muddy ditch. The experience left him with a weakness in his chest, and he was advised by his doctors to seek warmer climes if he was to make any significant improvement. Egypt was considered an ideal place to visit.

Carnarvon soon became restless for a new activity that would both hold his interest and offer financial promise. Archaeology was suggested as a suitable and potentially profitable pastime, and Howard Carter—by then a Cairo art and antiquities dealer with an impressive 432 discoveries to his credit—was just the man to assist him.

The concession to excavate in the Valley of the Kings passed to Lord Carnarvon when Theodore Davis retired from the activity in 1914. Work began in February 1915 and was almost immediately interrupted by the outbreak of World War I, when Carter was attached to British Intelligence. The dig resumed in 1917, at which time Carter formulated a final plan to concentrate on a triangular area of the valley, defined by the previously discovered royal tombs of Rameses II, Rameses VI and Merenptah (see map, page 26). Working north to south, it was the search of this area that was almost complete when Richard Adamson was posted to Luxor.

* * * * * * * *

Today the Valley of the Kings today is neat and orderly, with signposted pathways and an air-conditioned rest-house where visitors can escape the overwhelming heat. But when Sergeant Adamson first arrived it was very different—a scene of utter desolation littered with piles of excavation debris. There was no shelter from the desert sun, except for two small tents and a marquee.

1 November 1922. We crossed the river early
and I began to wonder, "Where on earth is he taking
me?" There was a range of white sandy hills in the

25

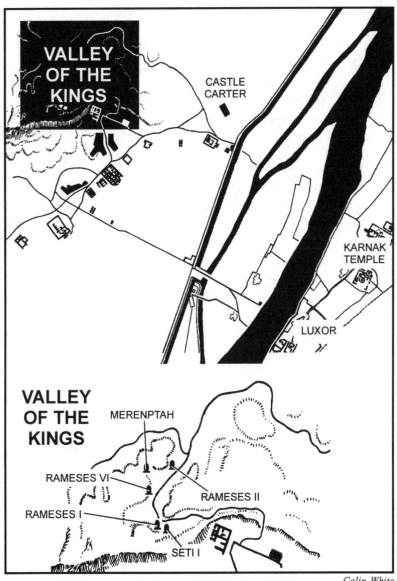

Colin White

*distance as we crossed the Nile. Mr. Carter said it
was Deir-el-Bahri and that behind the cliff was the
Valley of the Kings. It looked as if I were heading for
a desert wilderness. The "delights" of Luxor were
calling me back as I clambered up the steps of the
quay the other side, where a battered old Ford was
waiting, its driver in no particular hurry to get us
anywhere, and I was in no particular hurry to go
(except back over the Nile again, and pretty quick).*

*The car was loaded up with a hamper and
supplies. Then Mr. Carter and I were off up the dusty
track where we soon drove through fields with crops
of lush green vegetation on either side of us. The
fellahin were busy before it got too hot, labouring
away at their tasks. The strange irrigation systems
(or "shadufs") looked to me like tottering sticks
resembling wigwams, with animal skins full of water
hanging from them. They were worked by a lever
that would regulate the water flow into the
irrigation channels. The precious liquid was carefully
controlled so the minimum amount would create
the maximum result. The abundant crops proved it
worked, too. These shadufs were everywhere
creating a riot of green wherever I looked.*

*Later, though, we appeared to enter "boulder"
country as all around us seemed to become stark,
white and dust laden. The heat the rocks gave off
was intense and there was not even a breath of wind
to lessen the parched scorching conditions.
Mr. Carter seemed quite at ease, however, and
pointed out his house [popularly named "Castle
Carter"] up on a rise as we passed by. I thought to
myself, "He lives out here?"*

*At one point, the poor old Ford engine spluttered
to a halt. We climbed out and drank coffee,
thoughtfully provided by the hotel. It went down*

Elaine Edgar

"Castle Carter" at Elwat-el-Dibun, near the entrance to the Valley of the Kings

well while we were waiting for the engine to cool down. But the cliffs were beginning to close in on me by now as we continued still further inland. Mr. Carter announced with what I can only describe as the understatement of the century, "Of course, there is not much social life out here." I could not have cared less. I intended to load up this damned equipment and get it and myself out of this hell hole as soon as I possibly could. Yesterday would not have been soon enough!

Then the bombshell dropped when Mr. Carter mentioned that about a week should see the site cleared. "You mean, sir, I'll have to come over here each day?" Even as I said it, I knew what his answer was going to be, and my heart sank down into my boots.

The driver lurched the vehicle sharply to the right and we entered the Valley of the Kings where the cliff face towered above us. Even though there were some half dozen Egyptian workmen busy shovelling sand and rubble near to where we stopped, the sense of isolation was all around. An eerie feeling of loneliness came over me, and I shivered despite those 100 degrees-plus temperatures.

The hissing of the old car engine brought me back to reality with a jolt. I was not going to stray far from that old banger—it was my only means of escape and I fully intend to escape. I am not stopping here one minute longer than I have to …

"You will sleep here," Carter announced as they crouched beneath the rolled-up flaps that formed the entrance to the marquee. The canvas dwelling was empty but for rush mats on the floor, two stretcher-like cots and a trestle table.

"What about food?" gasped the astonished soldier, who had assumed he would be staying in Luxor.

"I'll have some sent up to you," was Carter's reply, which left Richard wondering whether he might not prefer to take his chances in Cairo after all. His first impulse was to start walking back to Cairo right away.

As Carter sat finishing his lunch that day, with the young soldier sitting beside him, he was still convinced there was something to be found. Around 200,000 tons of sand and rubble had been moved in the course of those 10 long years he had been working the site. A world war had raged seriously close too, but in the end it was of little interest to the workmen of the ancient burial site. Even though the excavations had been briefly suspended, another four years passed and still nothing substantial had been discovered.

Howard Carter's meeting with Lord Carnarvon had been exacting during those last days. Richard recalled,

> ... I can imagine what it must have felt like.
> After all that time, money and effort, only to be
> defeated by the unwillingness of the terrain to yield
> its crop ...

As Richard accustomed himself to his new surroundings, he questioned Carter about his search of the valley. "Have you worked here long, sir?" Richard asked.

"On and off for years. Like to see inside one of the tombs?" Carter asked his unwilling guest.

"Very well, sir," came Richard's grudging reply.

Richard followed Carter down the long, stone passageway into the bowels of the man-made cavern. It was the tomb of Rameses VI. The archaeologist was in his element as he explained to his latest recruit that it was of vital importance for the body to rest undisturbed in the place constructed for it. It was equally important for the deceased to be fully provisioned for every known need. But the magnificence of the items with which pharaohs provided themselves for their afterlife caused their eventual undoing. Within a few generations, their tombs had been sacked and the complete site eventually abandoned. Carter later elaborated:

> ". . . Strange sights The Valley must have seen
> and desperate the ventures that took place in it.
> One can imagine the plotting for days beforehand,
> the secret rendezvous on the cliff by night, the
> bribing or drugging of the cemetery guards, and
> then the desperate burrowing in the dark, the
> scramble through a small hole into the burial-
> chamber, the hectic search by a glimmering light

for treasure that was portable, and the return home
at dawn laden with booty[1] . . ."

As Howard Carter and Richard Adamson emerged from
the musty tomb of Rameses VI, it was as if by some peculiar
twist of fate that events would soon turn from a routine
clearing-up operation into something that changed their
lives forever.

* * * * * * *

---

1. *The Tomb of Tut-ankh-Amen*, Vol. I, by Howard Carter
and A.C. Mace.

3

SLEEPING IN THE VALLEY OF THE KINGS

The long days passed and Richard Adamson continued to resent his exile in the valley, all for the sake of some old survey equipment. True to military form, he kept his thoughts on the matter to himself, but privately reflected:

> *1 November 1922. My first night in the Valley of the Kings, it seemed I was in two lands. I would doze off for a while and then jolt awake at the slightest noise, getting crosser by the hour. The night seemed endless too, and in the end, I gave up trying to sleep. It was like a night from hell.*
>
> *By first light I was up, dressed and already inspecting the equipment that had to be packed up and shipped back to Cairo. Abdul, one of the Egyptian workmen, brought me a cup of coffee before disappearing into a tent with the other*

workmen. His full name is Abdul el Maaboud, very grand I thought, but I just call him Abdul, my hearing being a bit off when it comes to Arabic pronounced in hurried tones. He forgave my ignorance—and made damn good coffee, too!

It gets dark around here very early. I think I will walk up the track. I am getting restless here and am starving hungry and ill-tempered this evening.

Well, the fodder finally arrived. I sometimes forget that the Egyptians eat late and guess I must learn to adjust. It was good grub, though.

It's creepy here now, so quiet and still. I have read and re-read the Egyptian Gazette, written up my notes and must get some shut-eye soon if I can. Just hope that I do not have nightmares!

What had they hoped to find in this wilderness that would warrant habitation in this Godforsaken place. Surely nothing but a few old bones, perhaps, to get excited about, if indeed they had been successful and found anything worth having. Ah well, they have been digging long enough now and it must be frustrating to have to give up and go home with nothing.

The sooner I get back to reality the better. I cannot stand the thought of too many nights in this place...

During the afternoon of 3 November 1922, having resigned himself to his enforced stay in the Valley of the Kings, the young military policeman decided to explore his surroundings further. Little did he know that a drama was about to unfold, one that would command the attention of the world's press for decades to come.

Camera in hand, he climbed up a narrow trail above the site of a nearby tomb to look at the remains of some ancient workmen's huts. After taking a few photos, he started back down the steep path. Suddenly, he heard the sound of excited shouting from a small group of labourers who were clearing away rubble from the foundations of more old huts about 30 feet below him. Richard quickly proceeded down the slope to where the labourers had unearthed some boulders that looked distinctly out of place. A typewritten account recently found in Richard's belongings[1] recounts what transpired:

Griffith Institute, Ashmolean Museum, Oxford

*The ruins of workmen's huts above
the tomb of Rameses VI*

1. The entire document is contained in Appendix 3: Suitcase Treasures.

". . . On November 3rd, 1922, I was watching the workmen uncovering some ancient huts used during the building of the tomb of Rameses VI and noticed one large stone somewhat different from the rest. The workmen at once began to cover this up again, but I took some photos of the stone and position.

The workmen then began to dig away from this stone to a different area.

When Howard Carter arrived the following morning, I mentioned this to him and, as the photos had by then been developed and printed, we were able to pinpoint the spot. The stone was uncovered once more and proved to be the first of a flight of steps leading down into the hillside.

Griffith Institute, Ashmolean Museum, Oxford

Foundations above the stone staircase leading to the tomb of Tutankhamun

At the time, I was not clear as to why the workmen had tried to hide this stone, but later events gave the explanation.

(At one period, the Egyptian Government withdrew the extended concession and placed their own officials in charge, with disastrous results to the preservation of the treasures. After prolonged negotiations, Howard Carter was recalled and again took charge.)

It would appear that, had the tomb NOT been discovered on the morning of the 4th of November 1922, the concession (about to end) would not have been renewed. The Egyptians would then have recommenced excavations on the site of the original stone step—they had guessed what it was—and the Carnarvon-Carter expedition could never have claimed the discovery of the tomb . . ."

To Richard's untrained eye, the uncovering of the first few steps on 4 November was merely the discovery of rubble beneath rubble. But to Howard Carter, the potential was enormous, and he quickly put his crew to work at the location that had been identified.

As the Egyptian workers continued to clear away more and more debris, it became apparent to all present that they could well have found something important. Richard and Carter soon joined in, digging with their own hands and losing track of time as they excitedly continued to work until after sunset. In the soft glow of moonlight, the two Englishmen stared at the site in silence, then slowly walked back to the marquee.

After cleaning up and taking some refreshment, Richard bade the others goodnight. As he started to leave the tent,

Carter suddenly called to him, "I am afraid I'll have to ask you to sit out the night on the steps."

"Do what, sir?" Richard uttered in disbelief.

"I shall want you to spend the night on the steps," he repeated with a stern look in his eyes. Negotiation was clearly not an option.

Once again, Richard resigned himself to a strange and undesirable duty. He understood the importance of the order. They had uncovered 12 steps that day but had no idea what lay at the bottom of the stairwell.

> *4 November 1922. Now that these steps leading down to who-knows-what have been uncovered, I have taken up residence at the top of them so I have a clear view down and all about me. I am a fairly light sleeper and have no doubt that all will be secure come morning. I don't much fancy camping at the bottom of the steps as it's pretty airless down there, and there is still a lot of rubble to be removed from round about. It is heaped all up the sides in drifts at the moment, but there is now a clear enough path to walk up and down the steps. Even at the top of the steps it is a bit claustrophobic.*

> *I shudder when I think back to that first night I spent here in this valley. It was eerie! Everywhere it was so still, yet the slightest noise brought me straight on my feet and out looking around. Now I am even more alert and vigilant than ever.*

> *The desert seems to come alive at night—at least in my mind. Perhaps it is when I am most vulnerable, exhausted from the day's heat—and now with only two blankets to cover my limbs and torso this night. Tiny creatures slither about over the rubble, sometimes dislodging a stone in their endeavours to find a morsel to eat. There are snakes*

and scorpions, of course, which are not exactly my idea of perfect company, and I take any precaution necessary against them. The mosquitoes are not so busy in the cooler months, but I still have to be wary and cover up wherever possible ...

Guarding the staircase that night proved both long and difficult. Richard's imagination ran wild at the thought of what might have transpired on and below those steps in the past, and also at what lay ahead.

The next day, 5 November, the excavations continued, revealing a large wooden lintel and the upper portion of a door. The door was sealed with plaster which bore the unmistakable ancient imprints signifying a necropolis. More rubble was cleared to expose a further two steps. At the end of the day Carter determined that the door and its insignia were consistent with the 18th pharaonic dynasty—the time of Horemheb, Akhenaten and ... Tutankhamun.

Carter felt obliged to inform Lord Carnarvon of the developments before proceeding any further. He laid wooden planks and tarpaulins across the opening, then distributed piles of the evacuated loose material over the planks. This would help protect and disguise the site until Carnarvon arrived.

"I suppose this will put paid to Luxor completely," Richard quipped when the camouflaging task was completed.

Carter tried to console him with words of encouragement, "Come on, cheer up," then added, "Is there anything else you will need?" Richard quickly prepared a list of items which included a "decent" gramophone, records, some military issue, books and confectionery "as a start."

"Your job is now security," Carter advised his uniformed assistant later that evening. "I don't have to tell you how important it is. Good night, Richard. It's been a wonderful day." "Yes, sir," were the only words Richard could find. Security confirmed that the end of his desert ordeal was farther away than he had ever considered.

Carter invited his former assistant, Arthur Callender, to join him in the excavation. Callender was more than pleased to be reunited with his old friend and arrived in the valley around 9 November.

A frustrating two weeks later, Lord Carnarvon arrived in Luxor with his 21-year-old daughter Lady Evelyn Herbert and work was immediately restarted. Howard Carter gave credit to Richard for "looking after things very well in the valley," thus enabling Carter to "go off and organise other things prior to their visit."

P. North

The entrance to the tomb of Pharaoh Tutankhamun

Griffith Institute, Ashmolean Museum, Oxford

*The Valley of the Kings as it appeared
in the 1920s. The tomb of Tutankhamun
is behind and below the stone wall
(erected by Callender)*

By 24 November, the stairwell had been completely cleared. Uncovering the last two steps—16 steps in total—allowed the base of the door to be inspected. To Carter's ultimate joy, he found seal impressions of the Royal Necropolis and of the cartouche of Pharaoh Tutankhamun. The door was removed to reveal a long passageway, roughly 6 feet wide by 7 feet tall and, once more, filled with rubble.

The events that followed are recorded in Richard's typewritten notes: [2]

> ". . . After the flight of steps had been uncovered, a sealed doorway was found at the bottom which showed signs of having been opened and sealed up again. This door was removed to reveal a long passage filled with rubble and chippings. It was some thirty feet long. This was cleared to reveal another sealed doorway, again with the signs of having been opened and resealed.
>
> [On 26 November] Before removing this door, Howard Carter made a test to determine the nature of the air on the other side. He made a small hole in the top left-hand corner and inserted a lighted candle.
>
> We stood and watched as the flame flickered for a moment and then became a steady flame. Howard Carter then looked inside.
>
> The silence was intense until Lord Carnarvon broke the silence and called out, 'Can you see anything, Carter?' 'Yes,' was the reply, 'Wonderful things, wonderful things.' He stepped down and then Lord Carnarvon, who had by then been handed

---

2. The entire document is contained in Appendix 3: Suitcase Treasures.

a torch, stepped up and looked. His face was almost white as he stepped down and the others took their turn to look. Eventually the torch was handed to me and I stepped up and looked inside.

I do not know what I expected to see, but most certainly the sight took my breath away. As I moved the torch around, details of the vault emerged. It appeared to be full of objects the like of which no man had ever seen or was likely to see again . . ."

* * * * * * * *

4

BEYOND THE SIXTEEN STEPS

Howard Carter eloquently described his thoughts and feelings about what they found on 26 November 1922. His original notes were typed by Richard Adamson and were eventually absorbed into the official, published account of the discovery, *The Tomb of Tut-ankh-Amen*, by Howard Carter and Arthur C. Mace. Richard's written account[1] of the find also absorbs text from Carter's original notes and includes the following text:

> ". . . I quote from the notes Howard Carter sent to the Cairo Museum at the time: 'I suppose most excavators would confess to a feeling of awe when they break into a chamber closed and sealed by

---

1. The entire document is contained in Appendix 3: Suitcase Treasures.

pious hands so many centuries ago. For the moment, time as a factor in human life has lost its meaning. Three thousand, four thousand years maybe have passed and gone since human feet last trod the floor on which you stand and yet, as you note the signs of recent life around you, the half-filled bowl of mortar for the door, the blackened lamp, the finger mark upon the freshly painted surface, the farewell garland dropped upon the threshold—you feel it might have been but yesterday. The very air you breathe, unchanged throughout the centuries, you share with those who laid the mummy to its rest. Time is annihilated by little intimate details such as these, and you feel an intruder.'

As I looked into the vault, what most attracted attention were three huge couches in the form of animals, uncanny and grotesque, covered in gold. My gaze kept constantly returning to these objects as if drawn to them by a magnet. All around in utter profusion were chests, vases, shrines (from the open doors of one peered the head of a snake), boxes, chariots, thrones, chairs, miniature statues and everywhere, the glint of gold. The mind would not register what the eye could see. At the other end of the vault were two life-sized statues in black, overlaid in gold, facing each other like sentinels, gold-kilted, gold sandalled, carrying mace and staff, upon their foreheads the royal emblems of the sacred Cobra and Vulture.

We could, however, see no mummy and then we noticed that between the two statues was another sealed doorway. The explanation could only mean that this was only the threshold of the discovery, that behind that door would be found another chamber even more wonderful than that which we were now looking at and, in that chamber, in all the magnificent panoply of death would be found the Pharaoh . . ."

Carter described that day as ". . . the day of days, the most wonderful that I have ever lived through, and certainly one whose like I can never hope to see again."[2]

Even with all the splendours of the tomb etched into the intruders' minds, Richard Adamson sensed there was one more detail to be arranged: "Richard, this is only the beginning. You will have to remain on guard again tonight." And for the first time, Richard wholeheartedly agreed.

The next day, Carter, Carnarvon, Lady Evelyn, Callender and Adamson all entered the tomb for the second time, only to be overwhelmed by its contents again. To Carter, the find was the reward for a lifetime of toil, and he could not help but be consumed by mental imagery. Again, from Richard's notes:

> ". . . It was an uncanny feeling, as if we were in the presence of someone who, although dead, was still alive and watching. You seemed to inherit almost at once the belief of those long dead Egyptians that they do not die but live on again in the spirit of their Gods . . ."[3]

Hiding behind the treasures were signs that they had so far breached only an "antechamber" in a tomb complex of undetermined size.

On the northern wall, a large sealed doorway was evident between the "two life-sized statues in black, overlaid in gold." Once again, the unbroken seals of the Royal Necropolis and

---

2. *The Tomb of Tut-ankh-Amen*, by Howard Carter and A.C. Mace, Vol. I, London: 1923.
3. The entire document is contained in Appendix 3: Suitcase Treasures.

of the Pharaoh Tutankhamun were visible, indicating that somewhere behind the obstruction was the burial place of the ancient king.

At the southern end of the western wall, another sealed doorway was present with an open tomb-robbers' hole at its base. A cursory investigation through the hole revealed that behind this door was a smaller room (or "annexe") also crammed with "wonderful things."

It was immediately clear to Carter that the magnitude of the discovery demanded that a metal gate be fabricated to supplement the wooden one already being installed at the foot of the stairwell. It would also be necessary to empty the antechamber of its contents and to commence preservation work before the site could be explored further. He would need large quantities of packing materials and other supplies. His existing staff had nowhere near the expertise or resources necessary to adequately document, protect and preserve the tomb and its store.

A journey to Cairo allowed Carter to organise manpower and matériel. His requests for assistance met with predictable success. The New York Metropolitan Museum of Art provided Arthur Mace (an assistant curator and expert record keeper), Harry Burton (photographer), Lindsley Hall and Walter Hauser (architectural draughtsmen), and from Cairo came Alfred Lucas (chemist and conservator). In addition, Professor James Breasted (historian) and Dr. Alan Gardiner (philologist) were on call to lend their expertise as and when needed, and Lord Carnarvon had obtained clearance from the military authorities in Cairo to formalise Sergeant Adamson's role as security "officer."

By 23 December, the team had assembled in the valley, and the provisions from Cairo had arrived, including a mile of wadding, 32 bales of calico, crates, boxes, photographic

THE EASTERN TELEGRAPH COMPANY, LIMITED.

Thanks message discovery colossal and need every assistance could you consider loan of burton in recording in time being costs to us immediate reply would oblige every regards carter Continental Cairo

(above)   One of Carter's requests for assistance
(below)   Lythgoe's response

Form for Deferred Plain Language Telegrams.
E. T. Co. : LONDON.

Dec. 7. 1922.

To Receiver's Name LC Carter, Hotel Continental, Cairo

Only too delighted to assist in every possible way. Please call upon Burton and any other members of our staff. Am cabling Burton to that effect.

Lythgoe.

49

(l-r)
Mace,
(a guest),
Callender,
Lady Evelyn,
Carter,
Carnarvon,
Lucas,
Burton

Times Newspapers Limited

materials, chemicals—and the wind-up gramophone and other items on Richard's shopping list. The steel gate was immediately installed at the junction of the passageway and the antechamber. The meticulous work that was about to commence would take nearly 10 years to complete.

> *23 December 1922. The supply truck has arrived, including a few goodies for me. I cannot believe that I now have the use of my very own gramophone and a few records to go at. Although I only have three records to enjoy, I shall celebrate tonight after supper. I can play the music full blast, and no one can complain about the noise. I shall have my very own parade of Aida. This whole valley will reverberate with the sounds, the instruments shall sing, and the drums will roll. I will have my very own amphitheatre resounding with a symphony of spirits that will march through the Valley of the Kings, leaving an echo ringing down the years ...*

Nearby empty tombs were commissioned as storage areas and laboratories. On 27 December, the first object (item 21) was transferred from the tomb of Tutankhamun to the laboratory that was formerly the burial place of Seti I:

> *27 December 1922. A painted box, very beautiful, was the first object to be removed from the Antechamber. My job here is vital now as these objects are beyond price. I have to stay alert at all times, but have come to rely on the odd cat-nap when Mr. Carter is not at the site and only then if it is safe to do so. The pace is hotting up and even I am beginning to feel a sense of anticipation as each day passes ...*

Around the first week of January 1923, with many of the antechamber items temporarily lodging in other kings' tombs, Carter again concerned himself with the matter of tomb security. Richard was by now patrolling the area in civilian clothing, with his revolver concealed and an umbrella on his shoulder. His protective duties had been supplemented by contingents from the Egyptian Govt. Antiquities Guard and a detachment of soldiers provided by the Mudir of Kena, but Carter felt a trustworthy presence within the tomb was also necessary. "Richard, there is now enough room for you to take your bed down into the chamber."

> *5 January 1923. Tonight I am expected to move kit and caboodle downstairs. I had slowly become accustomed to the desert nights, but now even those are to be denied me as the "discovery" has become big business and my services are required elsewhere, namely underground ...*

That evening, Richard bade Carter a terse "goodnight," then descended the 16 steps, armed with three blankets, a book, his trestle camp bed and his revolver. Locking the metal gate behind him, Richard read himself to sleep. He had refused Carter's offer of a night light, content with a candle to read by.

He awoke at 4 a.m. the next morning in the company of the two Royal Ka statues and the remaining treasures. "What on earth am I doing here?" he wondered.

That evening in the marquee, Adamson pondered his new quarters and the two black and gold roommates. He approached Carter and his team of experts asking, "Those two big statues, sir, what are they, and why don't you move them out?" Carter lectured Richard on ancient Egyptian beliefs, explaining that the statues were the keepers of the pharaoh's soul during mummification and thereafter acted as protectors of his shrine. "It would have been a queer old surprise if I had awoken to find the blighters bending over

Griffith Institute, Ashmolean Museum, Oxford

*The northern wall of the antechamber,
showing the sealed doorway with Ka statues
and other treasures in original locations*

me!" As the assembled experts and scholars burst into laughter, Richard vowed never to ask such a "bloody stupid question" again.

The answer to the mystery of what lay behind the northern sealed doorway was scheduled for 17 February, although evidence suggests that the archaeologist and his benefactor were already privy to this knowledge. There would be two "opening" ceremonies: one for the academic/ archaeological hierarchy, and one for visiting dignitaries, including members of the Belgian Royal Family.

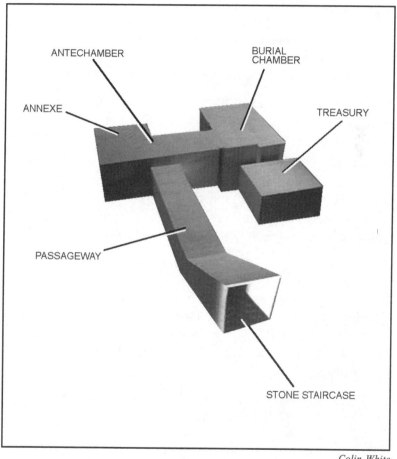

ANTECHAMBER

BURIAL
CHAMBER

ANNEXE

TREASURY

PASSAGEWAY

STONE STAIRCASE

Colin White

Layout of the tomb

16 February 1923. There is much excitement about the next phase of the project—expectation is running high. I will have to keep my wits about me tonight. I cannot be expected to stop down there for long periods as the air is quite foul after a full day's work and it is only a small place, really cramped, no room to turn around. From what I can see of it, quite uninspiring, too. I cannot understand what all the fuss is about at the moment, but we'll soon see...

At the first ceremony, the door was carefully removed to reveal a smaller chamber which housed a large gilt shrine. One wall of this "burial" chamber was formed into a rectangular arch which led to a further room, the "treasury," which contained the undisturbed traditional funerary items of a deceased ancient Egyptian King. Tutankhamun had been found. The Hon. Mervyn Herbert (Lord Carnarvon's half-brother) recorded in his 1922-1923 journal:

". . . Porch [Lord Carnarvon] and Evelyn and I started in his Ford, and after we had been going a few minutes, he said that it would really be alright [to join the tour] and he could quite well fit me in the tomb while it was being opened. Then he whispered something to Evelyn and told her to tell me.

This she did under the strictest promise of secrecy—it is a thing I would never give away in any case and it is one which I think ought not to be known, at any rate not at present. Here is the secret. They had both already been into the second chamber.

After the discovery, they had not been able to resist it. They had made a small hole in the wall, which they afterwards filled up again and climbed through. She described to me very shortly some of the extraordinary wonders I was soon to see . . .

The work proceeded and eventually he [Carter] got an opening big enough to let people through. He went in, then Porch and then eventually all of those who were there . . . When old General Maxwell went in at the official opening he got stuck, poor old fellow, and it took four men pushing and pulling to get him out again—which was eventually done with a noise like a champagne cork and with injury to what he wrongly described as his chest . . .

It was very hot and stuffy in the tomb and in spite of the thrilling excitement of it all, we were most of us glad to get into the air again. But I only heard of one person who didn't enjoy it, a coon who was heard to say that it had been a rotten uncomfortable day, and he couldn't think why he had been such a fool as even to have left his club in Cairo . . .

Porch, poor old fellow, was nervous like a naughty schoolboy, fearing that they would discover that a hole had already been made . . . The last I saw of the old fellow was in the hall of the Winter Palace Hotel talking to Maxwell, Merton the *Times* correspondent, and others. I had said my goodbyes more than once. Maxwell had said to me that Porch ought to go to Aswan as he needed a rest. I agreed that he was tired, although I don't think more so than was reasonably to be expected . . ."

Lord Carnarvon never reached Aswan. At the pinnacle of this triumph, his failing health demanded that he relocate to Cairo, where he died in a hotel bedroom in early April 1923. Among those in attendance were his wife Lady Almina, his son Lord Porchester, and his friend and accomplice, Howard Carter.

18 April 1923. The mood here has been a mix of sadness and anticipation since the announcement of Lord Carnarvon's death. Mr. Carter is solemn of course, misses the old chap, even though they had quite a few arguments towards the end. I suppose new arrangements will now have to be made about this place. Who will be running the show now I wonder?

In any case, I am going to be kept really busy next month as it is hoped to have some of the artifacts shipped off to the Cairo Museum ...

Griffith Institute, Ashmolean Museum, Oxford

(left) Howard Carter and (right) Arthur Callender preparing the Ka statues for transportation (the golden shrine is visible behind Callender)

The threat of damage to the fragile artifacts during shipment to Cairo was immense. The 450-mile distance from Luxor to Cairo posed its own risks, whether that distance was covered by rail or by boat. But by far the greatest concern was the movement of the tons of priceless objects from the Valley of the Kings to Luxor's West Bank—a stretch of around 5 miles.

Eventually, it was decided only safe and proper that the treasures of the boy-king be moved along the River Nile to Cairo. Furthermore, the precarious trip from the valley to the river bank would be effected by Décauville railway, a crude and slow, yet effective, means of manually transporting large and heavy loads over relatively short distances using

Times Newspapers Limited

The first crates travel through the valley for shipment to the Cairo Museum

portable railroad sections. Small railway trucks loaded with the priceless items were manually pushed to the limit of the tracks. The rear sections of track were then moved to the front and the individual wagons were pushed ahead again, and so on.

Although each batch of inventory took two days to complete its journey to the Nile by this method, no damage or losses were incurred. While Richard was busy overseeing the 50 labourers employed to progress the crated items to the West Bank, work continued on record keeping, preservation, packaging and investigation of the burial chamber and treasury. When the exhausted security officer returned from each journey, his last action of the day would be to imprison himself in the subterranean dungeon that had become the romantic and cultural event of the century to the outside world.

Within the burial chamber, the large gilt shrine was dismantled to reveal a similar but slightly smaller unit within. When that item was opened, a third rectangular gilt shrine manifested itself, and after that, a fourth. Within the fourth shrine was an exquisitely sculpted quartzite sarcophagus: the final resting place of an ancient king.

To Carter it signified the last episode in his long search for Pharaoh Tutankhamun. To Richard, it confirmed that many more nights would be spent in claustrophobia.

* * * * * * * *

5

LIKE
RUSSIAN DOLLS

The sarcophagus was opened on 12 February 1924. The lid alone weighed over 1¼ ton and required the assistance of specially improvised lifting gear because of the lack of space in the burial chamber. Peering in, Carter first observed an ancient shroud and amulets. He carefully pulled back the cloth to reveal a golden effigy of the Pharaoh. The immediate temptation to open the coffin was tremendous, but it was wisely resisted. There were other matters to attend to first—matters that were causing much disquiet in the valley.

12 February 1924. At last! The lid of the sarcophagus has been finally lifted after much effort all round. A mammoth task, it has revealed a coffin, but there is great unrest here at the moment and the tension rises by the hour. The natives are getting restless as they say. I am keeping my nose well-and-truly out and my head well-and-truly down until the situation is resolved! ...

Under the terms originally negotiated with the Egyptian Government, the concession passed to Lord Carnarvon's wife, Lady Almina. However, the Egyptian authorities saw the death of Lord Carnarvon as being an ideal time to take control of the project. Howard Carter was under increasing pressure to bow to the will of the Egyptian Government, in particular the Ministry of Public Works and the Department of Antiquities. This affected progress in the tomb and enraged Carter to the extent that in mid-February he sent a dispatch to Cairo advising that no further work would be performed at the site until he was once again granted autonomy. In essence, the expedition went on strike.

Two days later, the Egyptian authorities responded by cancelling the Carnarvon concession and barring Carter and his team from the tomb.

15 February 1924. We are locked out! What the hell is going on? I have been given leave, but none of us knows what is to happen next. It appears that the local authorities have taken over. Just when we were getting so near, first the strike then this lock-out. It is just not fair after everyone's hard work, and so very disappointing. Well, that is it for the duration. Just have to wait, like the rest, for "word" ...

The strike and lockout had occurred so swiftly that there was no opportunity to leave the site in a tidy fashion. In particular, a unique and priceless pall was left outside the laboratory, and the lid of the sarcophagus was left hanging precariously in mid-air, suspended only from the tackle that was used to lift it.

An exhausted Carter returned to England to recuperate for a few weeks, then sailed to the United States of America where an extensive lecture tour awaited him. For the remainder of 1924, the expedition team, as such, was ostensibly unemployed. With his security duties now much reduced, Richard Adamson was granted a long overdue but short leave of absence. He returned to his homeland and married his old sweetheart Lillian "Kate" Penfold in Portsmouth on 24 December 1924.

The excavation site was not completely abandoned by the team though. After his short visit to England, Richard returned to the Valley of the Kings. He monitored the outdoor movements of the Egyptian usurpers by daytime and enjoyed his gramophone records, books and the fresh night air during the hours of darkness. Carter had instructed Richard not to obstruct or interfere with the Egyptians, but merely to "observe things." The authorities took an extensive inventory of the artifacts, and it was at this time that an apparent anomaly was discovered—some items were missing. The brunt of the accusations were levelled at the absent Carter, who firmly denied removing anything except for shipment to the Cairo Museum.

If Carter, Carnarvon and/or others had removed artifacts surreptitiously, it was done without Richard's knowledge. "While our work was in progress I slept all night, every night, at the top of the steps and later in the burial chamber itself. Anybody going in or out would have had to step right over me," Richard always insisted, which ruled out the possibility of clandestine night-time visits. Yet there is evidence in the archives at the Metropolitan Museum of Art and elsewhere that gives credence to the accusations of impropriety. Furthermore, as Howard Carter was the director of operations at the site, he would not have to appear as a thief in the night to perform such acts.

Indeed Richard, normally easygoing, would in his later years become visibly angry at the suggestion that Carter took, for example, a perfume box and a chalice. "I was the only person to stay with Carter during the entire period of excavation. He was abrupt and liable to be quarrelsome, but he was the most correct man I ever knew. It was lucky for the world that it was Carter who discovered the tomb. If someone else had found it, things would have been different. "These treasures belong to Egypt and should stay in Egypt," Carter often declared.

The dispute over the concession lasted until mid-January 1925. The tomb had been out of bounds to Carter and his team of experts for nine months. When Carter returned to the site and re-entered the burial chamber, he found to his relief that the lid of the sarcophagus was resting on wooden planks laid across the body of the piece. Sadly, when they reached the laboratory, the pall had not been taken inside and was completely ruined by the elements.

> *October 1925. Well, here we all are again.*
> *Mr. Carter finally got permission to restart our work*
> *here in the valley and has been hard at it ever since.*
> *Security seems to have been well maintained inside*
> *the various tombs by the Egyptian guards during the*
> *shutdown. Now I appear to have become "minder to*
> *a pharaoh." Strange, but true . . .*

Almost the entire year was spent planning and executing the exploration of the sarcophagus. Slowly, the archaeological team drifted back to the site. On 13 October, the golden coffin that had so amazed the archaeologists before the interruption was opened to reveal another within, this time wrapped in a linen shroud on which were found garlands of flowers. Howard Carter suggested the flowers were likely placed there by Tutankhamun's young queen as a farewell tribute. Ten days later that coffin was opened to

P. North

Detail of the solid gold inner coffin

reveal a third magnificently sculpted coffin made from 2,448 pounds of pure, solid gold.

> *23 October 1925. After much excitement the lid of the coffin was raised, only to reveal another one within—and inside that, yet another. A bit like Russian dolls, this lot . . .*

On 28 October, the lid of the innermost coffin was raised. Within lay the mummified remains of the Pharaoh, crowned with the renowned gold mask.

> *28 October 1925. Did my eyes deceive me? Am I dreaming, or what? I just cannot comprehend what I have seen here today. It is too magnificent for words, and the sheer scope of what I have been witnessing here is just beginning to dawn on me.*

P. North

P. North

The famous golden mask of Tutankhamun

The lid of the inner coffin was removed to reveal a mummy—at last! All those treasures, the golden shrines and artifacts of superb craftsmanship, the wonderful death mask of the mummy and everywhere it seems, we have encountered such splendour, the human eye just cannot take it all in.

I have already moved my camp bed down beside the sarcophagus and in between the narrow space and the tomb wall. I can just get into bed by edging my rear backwards, from the foot of the bed, but it's a struggle. An alarm has been rigged up, so all I need to do, if I get into difficulties, is flick a switch and a light will flash up above ground. Security is really tight of course, since all the treasures have been discovered, but I have a revolver at the ready, should I need it.

I will admit to feeling very strange down here, cooped up all alone, just me and the mummy. I sleep just inches away from it and it's damn eerie. I keep imagining all sorts of things. My brain is running away with mad ideas, exploding in a riot of daft thoughts. Then common sense takes over again and I tell myself not to be so bloody silly. It's just a job after all, and someone has to do it ... but why me? I've been escort and bodyguard to some interesting people, but this has got to be a one off!

I have been here in the valley of the dead for three years now. During that time my sleeping quarters have moved further and further down into this hell-hole, and closer and closer to this dead king. I am actually beginning to feel entombed myself. It is becoming increasingly difficult for me to imagine what a normal life would be like now. Prison must be like this. Incarceration. At least prisoners have living souls to shout at through their cell bars, but here, there's just mummy and me!

Only when I wind up the old gramophone and those overtures echo their scratchy yet moving tones around this valley do I feel alive again (I don't think the locals are very much impressed with it all, though). The rest of the time, someone has to pinch me, or else I could honestly believe I was dreaming all of this. The music whisks away the cobwebs of my exile, replacing the silence and loneliness of this existence with real, honest-to-goodness "life" again.

I have not been able to find the answers to all the questions in my mind, but I do know that nothing that follows in my life will ever come close to this. I must catch it all, remember it all, savour it all!...

Sergeant Adamson's military service engagement ended in 1925. He was now Mr. Richard Adamson, the civilian. As he had earned the trust and respect of the archaeological team, he continued his security duties in the valley. By this time, the New York Metropolitan Museum of Art had officially taken over financing the project from the Carnarvon estate.

Dr. Douglas Derry (a professor of anatomy at the Egyptian University) and Dr. Saleh Bey Hamdi (Director of Sanitary Services, Alexandria) performed an autopsy on the remains of the Pharaoh. Despite the legends regarding ancient Egyptians having perfected the art of body preservation, Tutankhamun's remains were found to be in extremely poor condition. They established little more than the age of the dead king: Tutankhamun had died around the age of 18. The cause of death could not be determined.

In late 1926, Carter turned his attention to the treasury which they had discovered, and surveyed for two days, back in February 1923. At that time, it had been deemed appropriate to temporarily block the entrance with wooden

P. North

The contents of the canopic chest:
four alabaster jars with stoppers exquisitely
carved in the form of the Pharaoh

boards for protection. The principal item in the treasury was a large gilded canopy cloaking a gilt box. The box in turn contained the canopic chest housing four receptacles which held the viscera of the departed Pharaoh. "Like those Russian dolls again," Richard quipped.

When the treasury was emptied about a year later, work started on the annexe. This small room was in far greater disarray than any of the other chambers. It was apparent to Carter that the room had been violated by ancient robbers on two separate occasions. The rigid and meticulous procedure of photographing, cataloguing, preserving and packaging continued until the annexe was emptied of its approximately 300 items. Only then, on 10 November 1930, was Richard relieved of his tomb vigil duties.

10 November 1930. The final objects have been removed from the tomb, and the team are busy processing these last artifacts. I continue to help with Mr. Carter's field notes where I can, and these have given me a real insight into current events at each turn.

I am indeed becoming a well-read and articulate fellow. I could hold my own on the subject of the tomb and its treasures. I have taken great interest in everything and been fascinated by the sheer quality of the craftsmanship of the ancient Egyptians. Such skills—unique to them. I have learned much here, but I still find it very difficult to understand just how they could produce such quality with what I imagine must have been basic tools and facilities. Their techniques appear to be second to none and truly worthy of admiration ...

Finally, two years later in the spring of 1932, the very last items were transferred to the west bank of the Nile for shipment to Cairo.

Spring 1932. We are all preparing to move out. I have announced to Mr. Carter that the last of the equipment is packed and ready for shipment to Cairo—a report I was originally scheduled to make 10 years ago!

It will not be long before I say goodbye to this place and set off for another life, one far from here. A stranger one there will never be, but part of me will always remain here in this place. Part of my soul has seeped into the sand and stone, and I know that I will never be quite the same for this experience.

Ron Slaughter

Entrance to the tomb of
Tutankhamun in 1996

Ron Slaughter

Today's epitaph: a modest acknowledgement to the
treasures that the tomb housed for thousands of years

* * * * * * * * *

6

THAT
DAMNED CURSE

Richard would frequently type up Carter's notes on site and was therefore very close to events as they happened. However, he was not the only informed person to record what actually transpired. As the following extracts from the journal of the Hon. Mervyn Herbert show, all was not plain sailing when it came to media coverage. As early as the official opening on 29 November 1922, the plague of reporters was threatening to compromise progress.

> " . . . The Sunday opening, although nominally small, was naturally a much bigger business. In the first place, the press men were hanging like vultures over the mouth of the tomb and there were a good many visitors, the Queen of the Belgians, the Allenbys and a good many others . . ."

Richard, being responsible for security measures, bore the brunt of the press attacks:

> *16 January 1923. I have nicknamed the press people "buzbies" as they are continually buzzing about in swarms and it seems an endless task to maintain any sort of order here.*
>
> *It has been worse this time. The visitors press like sardines into every nook and cranny. Back in November when we had the "official" opening of the Antechamber and Annexe we were saved from the buzbies' first reports, at least until afterwards. It has got to get easier now that Lord Carnarvon has signed a contract giving The Times full reporting rights. The buzbies will have to go on their way now and leave us all alone to get on with the job in hand—perhaps...*

Lord Carnarvon had sold exclusive reporting rights to the *London Times* (*The Times*) for £5,000 (plus a high percentage of revenues generated by *The Times* reselling the stories to other newspapers) about a week before the burial chamber was first opened. *The Times* correspondent Arthur Merton would be briefed daily by Carter or Callender usually in the comfort of a Luxor hotel. The remaining swarms of reporters had an extremely frustrating time competing with each other for a snippet of information or glimpse of things. To them, the biggest obstacle was the military policeman who at best offered little more than a polite rejection and, at worst, drove the point home with a clenched fist. In this way, it was assured that no information was disseminated to the general media before it had been published in *The Times*. This manoeuvre did not fare well with the media as Mervyn Herbert's journal confirms:

> ". . . Porch, I think, had a very worrying time at Luxor, not that he disliked it all. Some of it

amused him quite a lot. But the journalists were beyond belief. The prince of swine was, of course, Weigall who is only satisfactory in one way. He looks as complete a cad as he is. In the hotel where we all stayed, there were two groups of journalists, the sheep and the goats. The principal of the sheep was physically rather like one. Weigall and the rest were unutterable. They spied and lied and—well, as I have not seen it done.

Porch showed me a letter from Weigall saying that he had been asked to do reports on the tomb. He didn't much like the job, but he put himself entirely in Porch's hands. He would do whatever he liked. Porch told him about the agreement he had made with *The Times* and why he had been obliged to do so. The next thing was Weigall's series of venomous lies about Porch, about his having turned the whole thing into a commercial enterprise, and so on. Someday I hope that man will get a bad time, and I should like to be instrumental in giving it . . ."

Even with the *Times* agreement in place, there were about 200 reporters still sniffing around for information, not to mention hordes of tourists who had read and heard the reports. None were deterred by the fact that access to the valley from the ferry was mainly by donkey. Ironically, it was a journalist who came up with an idea which seemed to be a good solution to the media hassle and to Richard's security problems. The journalist in question, under pressure from his London office for an exclusive story, gave birth to the "curse of Tutankhamun," "the mummy's curse," *et al*. The curse warned that anyone who desecrated the Pharaoh's tomb would meet with a swift and horrible death. It was hoped that the macabre idea would keep the "riffraff and would-be tomb robbers" (as Richard often described the contemporary opportunists and treasure hunters) away for good. The curse not only made for sensational copy but also ensured that fewer reporters and tourists dared come near the place at night. Indeed, many journalists would prefer to patiently await news of developments from the safety of Luxor—or even beyond. Richard and other members of the expedition were at first more than pleased to allow the preposterous story to spread.

Although the curse was born of the press, its egg was fertilised by a series of unconnected events in Egypt and England at the time that the burial chamber was being explored. Carter's pet canary, normally heard chirping and whistling on the verandah at "Castle Carter," was rendered permanently silent by a cobra (the ancient symbol of Lower Egypt). This event was immediately construed as an evil omen.

A few months later, Lord Carnarvon was bitten on the cheek by a mosquito as he left the tomb. The following day, while shaving at the Winter Palace Hotel, he nicked the head of the bite with his razor. The infection spread, leading to blood poisoning and pulmonary pneumonia. He died in Cairo during the early hours of the morning of 5 April 1923, shortly after uttering the words, "I have heard the call. I am preparing."

At the very moment that Lord Carnarvon passed away, the entire city of Cairo was plunged into darkness by a total failure of the city's electricity system. Although the blackout lasted a mere five minutes, no technical fault was ever found to explain the phenomenon.

Perhaps even more uncanny was a report from Highclere Castle, England, Lord Carnarvon's family seat some 4,000 miles away. Simultaneous to the fifth Earl's passing and the

Ron Slaughter

Highclere Castle, England,
family home of the Earls of Carnarvon

Colin White

Grave of the fifth Earl of Carnarvon
at Beacon Hill, Highclere

Cairo power failure at 1:55 a.m., the family's pet terrier "Susie" howled, rolled over and died.

The press rose to the occasion by claiming that these escalating incidents had been ordained by "King Tut" to avenge the disturbance of his sacred remains.

Richard, the ever-practical Yorkshireman, had a more realistic outlook:

> *10 April 1923. Sad news has filtered in that his Lordship has passed away. Weird tales continue to circulate about curses and such rubbish; Lord Carnarvon was bitten by an insect, and died of blood poisoning. But anyway, the poor man had not been in the best of health; that's why he came here in the first place.*
>
> *It is such a pity that he will not see the results of his efforts. He had ploughed so much money into this project over the years and was so absolutely thrilled when we opened the antechamber, etc. Words actually failed him at one point . . .*

Newspapers refused to allow the curse to die. It sold copies. Stories abounded as to warnings of dire peril that Carnarvon had received. Even Richard reluctantly acknowledged a private conversation with Lady Evelyn wherein she confessed that her father had received at least three warnings from spiritualists. The most disturbing was from a Count Louis Hamon, or "Cheiro," who later recalled:

> ". . . As the vision faded away, the electric lamp again burned normally and I read aloud what I had written on the pad. It was nothing more or less than a warning to Lord Carnarvon.
>
> It was to the effect that on his arrival at the Tomb of Tut-Ankh-Amen he was not to allow any of the relics found in it to be removed or taken

away. The ending of the message was 'that if he
disobeyed the warning he would suffer an injury
while in the tomb—a sickness from which he would
never recover, and that death would claim him in
Egypt.' . . . " [1]

When the results of the 1925 autopsy on the remains of
Tutankhamun were released, the press once again embraced
the curse. The autopsy revealed that, "on the left cheek, just
in front of the lobe of the ear, is a rounded depression, the
skin filling it, resembling a scab." Newspapers around the
world were quick to identify this location with the place
where the mosquito had bitten Lord Carnarvon.

For years, in fact for decades, the press insisted on
attributing any death of a significant tomb attendee (and in
some cases would-be tomb attendee) to the "mummy's
curse." Eventually even Carter became tired of the issue and
denounced the media sensationalists as "mischievous,
unpardonable, mendacious and malicious." In *The Tomb of
Tut-ankh-Amen*, he wrote:

> ". . . The sentiment of the Egyptologist is not
> one of fear, but of respect and awe. It is entirely
> opposed to the foolish superstitions which are far
> too prevalent among emotional people in search of
> 'psychic' excitement . . ."

A page of typed notes found in Richard's suitcase, hand-
annotated "ISSUED TO THE PRESS IN 1934," addresses the
"curse" in sober reality. The page lists those present at the
official opening of the tomb (24-26 November 1922), the
opening of the inner chamber (17 February 1923), the
opening of the sarcophagus (3 February 1924) and the

---

1. *Real Life Stories: A Collection of Sensational Personal
Experiences*, by "Cheiro" (Count Louis Hamon), p 46.

examination of the mummy (11 November 1925)—a total of 40 people who were prime candidates for the curse. There follows a list of those amongst the 40 names who died between 1923 and 1934. The list is remarkably short and does not include canaries or dogs:

1923	Age Died	Year Died	Age Cause	
Carnarvon (Lord)	57	1923	57	Pneumonia
Garstin (Sir William)	74	1926	77	Natural causes
Mace (Arthur C.)	49	1928	54	Tuberculosis
Herbert (Mervyn)	41	1930	48	?
Bethell (Richard)	40	1931	48	Suicide (?)
Chast (Sir Charles)	59	1932	68	?
Lythgoe (Albert W.)	55	1934	56	Arterio-sclerosis

A second document lists a further 13 "victims," together with comments:

Woolf, Joel
English sportsman, Friend of Carnarvon's.
Sir Archibald Douglas Reid
X-ray expert who was going to take an X-ray but never saw the tomb.
Frederick Raleigh
X-ray expert who was going to take an X-ray but never saw the tomb.
Arthur E. P. Weigall
Press troublemaker who was never allowed in the tomb except with the public. Had no part in any way with tomb work.
Colonel Aubrey Herbert
Who was never in the tomb. Perhaps confused with his brother Mervyn.
Professor Lafleur of Magill University
Who came out to Egypt for his health. Was ill before he ever came to Egypt.
H.G. Evelyn White
Who never was in Egypt after the tomb was discovered.

Georges Benedite
> Arrived after the tomb was closed for the summer.
> Was never in it.

Professor Casanova
> If he ever was in the tomb it was as a tourist only.
> Had no connection with the work.

"Prince" Ali Fahmy Bey
> Murdered in the Savoy Hotel in London by his French
> wife. If he ever was in the tomb it was as a tourist.

Lord Westbury
> Whose son was Richard Bethell. He himself never saw
> the tomb. If he ever was in Egypt it was years before
> the tomb was discovered.

The boy who was run over by Lord Westbury's hearse.

Despite his monumental achievements, Howard Carter died an embittered, semi-forgotten man in his London home on 2 March 1939. A few desperate journalists, still thirsting for a new take on that special story, even attributed this

Colin White

Howard Carter's grave at
Putney Vale Cemetery, London

ludicrously late event to the "curse," although Carter had suffered from a form of cancer for nearly a decade, had seriously rejected the theory, and the tomb discovery was then some 20 years behind him.

Rather than become more objective, the list has become more preposterous. In 1966, Mohammed Ibraham died of a fractured skull after being hit by a car. His only connection with Tutankhamun was that, as Director of Egyptian Antiquities in Cairo, he had been campaigning to prevent the treasures from being displayed abroad.

Richard maintained throughout his long life that the curse was pure invention and that illnesses attributed to the curse were caused by fungi and bacteria in the tomb. He could always be relied upon to give logical explanations of "curse-induced deaths" to any oncomers. Indeed, the story of the curse was the one thing guaranteed to "get him going."

Even in 1972, workmen at the British Museum in London were sworn to secrecy over a foreman who dropped dead while the Tutankhamun Exhibition was being organised. In the 1920s, the curse was used to keep people away through fear. Half a century later, the fear was that the curse story would be successful.

* * * * * * *

7

TIME OF REFLECTION

Surrender yourself to silence
Immerse your soul in stillness.
Anthony Bales

W hen Richard Adamson returned from the Valley of the Kings in 1932, he suddenly found himself reunited with the western world after sleeping in an ancient tomb with the remains of an Egyptian pharaoh for so many years. He had only been granted three brief leaves of absence during his service in the valley, and the transition was a most difficult task for him.

To help with this transition, Richard immersed himself in his family. His wife Kate was a tender woman who lived by the philosophy of *speak no evil, do no harm to others*. His first two sons, Ronald and Edward, had spent the early years of their lives with no memory of their father but for the rare and brief visits when he was home on leave from Egypt. His third son Robert had been born in 1930 and did not meet his father until he was approximately two years old.

After a few years, Kate bore two more sons, Patrick and John. As a parent, Richard imposed a typically strict traditional British upbringing on his children, which contrasted strongly with his wife's gentle character. Although Kate was unassuming by nature, she persuaded Richard to keep silent about his stay in the Valley of the Kings. And so his own children grew up knowing nothing of his earlier adventures.

He soon returned to the perceived comfort of a regimented work environment, this time at the Admiralty Signals and Weapons Establishment in Portsmouth, England, as a coding officer. The precise nature of his work for the Admiralty was such that he was never able to discuss it, even with his family. However, family members recall him being collected from his home and being driven to his place of work at the Admiralty Dockyard. Little more is known about Richard's career during this period of his life.

photographer unknown

Richard Adamson in 1940

Shortly after the outbreak of World War II, he joined the Royal Air Force Volunteer Reserve while his wife worked in a garment factory. During the Battle of Britain, he manned a barrage balloon unit, part of the air defences that helped provide protection for the important Portsmouth shipbuilding industry and naval installations. A photograph taken in 1940 depicting the man in his Royal Air Force uniform has survived and is included here.

Richard had a few favourite pastimes. He read profusely, never forgetting the impression made upon him by the scholars he had known on site in Egypt. Another passion was general knowledge through the medium of quizzes and game shows. He also became very involved with the promotion of stage talent. The celebrated British ballad singer David Whitfield was one such recipient of Richard's efforts.

In 1964 Richard was forced to retire from the civil service on medical grounds stemming from his active service days in the trenches and "all that gas." This was a difficult period for him because he was not the type of man to remain idle. He threw himself deeper into his hobbies as a means of keeping busy. He would often reflect on his military career but remained loyal to his wife's request to be silent on the matter of his adventures in Egypt.

Kate Adamson died of cancer in 1967. The next generation of Adamsons were by then fully grown men with their own lives to lead. Richard suffered immensely from the loss of his wife and as a means of consolation decided to return to the remaining big interest in his life. He reflected on the great discovery and other events that he had been part of in his army days, and made tireless attempts to record whatever details he could for posterity. The results of his efforts lie in dusty and forgotten social, military and Egyptian

photographer unknown

*Richard Adamson
as he appeared in the 1950s*

photographer unknown

Kate Adamson

archives, no doubt yellow with age and never to surface again. He sent a multitude of letters, reports and other details of his adventures to the Department of Antiquities in Egypt, the Royal Military Police Museum, and even to the British Royal Family at Buckingham Palace. He campaigned fiercely to persuade Egyptian President Gamal Abdel Nasser to return the personal photographs Richard had taken with his camera during the tomb discovery period.

One day he decided he could no longer remain silent on his fascinating past. Never one to waste a moment, Richard Adamson set to with fervour, collecting together sufficient material to start giving lectures around the British Isles. He was by then a proud old soldier, always ready with a smile and a story for anyone who would care to listen. And listen they did—they even queued to listen.

* * * * * * * *

8

CENTRAL
STAGE

In 1968, a scientific team led by Professor R.G. Harrison, a forensic anatomist from the University of Liverpool, once again opened the coffin of Tutankhamun, hoping that technological developments since the "original" autopsy performed by Dr. Derry could throw more light on the ancient monarch's circumstances and demise. X-rays were taken and various tests were conducted in the tomb. The material was analysed later, and the results were sent to the Egyptian authorities. In essence, despite the many technological developments since the original examination 45 years earlier, very little was added to Derry's original findings. The age of Tutankhamun at death was confirmed, blood tests indicated that the young man was related to Pharaoh Akhenaten, and an anomaly towards the rear of the

Photographer unknown

*Pharaoh Tutankhamun, as
revealed during the 1968 study*

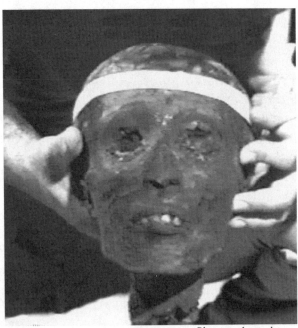

Photographer unknown

skull suggested a blow from a blunt instrument or a heavy fall as being the probable cause of death.

Richard thought that perhaps this new professional interest could counteract the low esteem with which the general public now held the discoverers. In January 1969, he wrote to the Department of Antiquities in Cairo regarding suggestions that the body of the Pharaoh had not been treated with due honour, respect and care by the excavation team. In particular, it had been suggested that the dismembered sections of the body indicated almost frantic activity to find more precious items. Although the exact content of Richard's letter to the Egyptian authorities is not known, he did receive this reply from Dr. Zaky Iskander, Director of Technical Affairs at the Department of Antiquities:

> ". . . When we opened the outermost gilt coffin on the 4th of December 1968 in the Valley of the Kings, we have found the mummy actually dismantled, i.e., the head, the arms and the feet separate from the trunk, and even the arms are dismantled into many pieces.
>
> The discoverer and his assistants of experts such as Dr. Derry and Lucas should not be blamed for this, since as you know the mummy was firmly fixed to the gold coffin.
>
> Also over the head, shoulders and a part of the chest was the gold mask which was stuck to the mummy and the bottom of the coffin by the same kind of resin. It was thus impossible to remove the jewellery or examine the interior of the skull and the other members of the body without dismantling some of its parts. Carter did not rewrap the mummy in the same manner as before, but merely put it on sand arranged as far as possible over sand in a long wooden box and introduced into the

outermost gilt coffin which was kept in the tomb inside the quartzite sarcophagus.

Lord Carnarvon could not have reached the mummy if he had actually entered the burial chamber before it was officially opened, since it was enclosed in four shrines, a stone sarcophagus whose lid could not be lifted up without removing the shrines, then in three coffins whose lids were so heavy that they found great difficulty in lifting them up.

The gold plate which should have covered the incision was not found inside the mummy as you mentioned, but only a Y-shaped amulet of sheet-gold and an oval gold plate were found at the left flank within the few outer bandages. The inside of the cavities of the body were not examined until now.

As to the brain, it is mentioned by Derry (*The Tomb of Tut-ankh-Amen*, vol. II, p. 226) that it was extracted through the nose and that the skull was empty except for some resinous material which had been introduced through the same route."

Richard always maintained that Lord Carnarvon and Howard Carter were innocent of the various charges that had been levelled during and after the discovery of the tomb of Tutankhamun. When Richard wrote to the Department of Antiquities, it was an attempt to lend support to the defence of the discoverers. He still felt loyalty to the team he had worked with all those years. He was angry that the media had continued to sway public opinion in favour of sensationalism, or "Tutmania" as it had become known, for over 45 years. It saddened him that such a rich, wonderful discovery was still being set upon in this fashion.

Fortunately, there were some who were genuinely interested in the facts. One day Richard received a written invitation from Buckingham Palace to attend H.R.H. Prince Charles at his study at Trinity College, Cambridge. Prince Charles, who was studying archaeology at the time, chatted with Richard for nearly four hours. "Prince Charles was interested and fascinated by everything I had to say to him. He told me it was the most fascinating thing he had heard," Richard recalled.

BUCKINGHAM PALACE

From: Squadron-Leader David Checketts, M.V.O.

13th December   PERSONAL

Dear Mr. Adamson,

    The Prince of Wales has asked me to write, and let you know how much he enjoyed listening to your account of the discovery, and the opening of Tutankhamen's Tomb.

    His Royal Highness greatly appreciated the time you gave to him, and sends his sincere thanks and best wishes.

    It is most kind of you to send the extracts from the diary of The late Honourable Mervyn Herbert, which I will return as soon as Prince Charles has finished reading them.

Yours sincerely,

Richard Adamson, Esq.

In July 1969, Richard became newsworthy in his own right when a Hampshire newspaper printed a full-page spread on his involvement in the original discovery of the tomb. On the death of draughtsman Lindsley Hall earlier that year, Richard had become the very last surviving member of that great archaeological excavation. Reluctant at first to appear in print (due in no small part to his past experiences with the press), he had ensured that what was going to be published was accurate.

The topic of the curse followed Richard wherever he went. On one occasion, he agreed to a BBC interview only to be told by the producer, "We don't want the truth, just the headlines that will come if you say there really is a curse."

In 1970, Richard went to Norwich for a TV interview on the topic and once again denied the existence of the curse. As he travelled from Norwich to Cambridge, he was injured when his taxi collided with a tractor. Richard was thrown from the taxi and narrowly escaped death when a passing vehicle missed him by inches. While in hospital recovering from his injuries, he was filmed by a camera crew. The ensuing footage was dubbed over with someone impersonating his voice to give the impression that, due to the car accident, Richard was now reconsidering his denial of King Tut's curse. "I've denied it over and over again, but it is so sensational that people want to believe it, no matter what you say. It's come down nearly half a century that way, and they still want to believe it," was Richard's typical response.

The only book to seriously acknowledge the depth of Richard Adamson's involvement with the discovery of the tomb was *Behind the Mask of Tutankhamen*, written by Barry Wynne and published in 1972. Richard worked extensively with the author, providing much of the detail and insight for which the work is noted.

*The Hampshire Telegraph
article, 31 July 1969*

He continued with lecturing on the subject of Tutankhamun's tomb, giving his recollections and views to packed houses wherever he went. The British Museum loaned him a valuable ancient Egyptian relic to display during his talks. It was an ornate necklace owned by Queen Hatshepsut, over 3,000 years old. The fact that Richard had been entrusted with this necklace lent much substance to his presentations.

I had heard about his lectures and read about the man who had slept in a tomb, guarding a pharaoh. I wanted to meet him as much for his having done such a thing and the courage that must have taken, as for my own fascination with the subject. At a young age, I had been set upon the road to that land by my mother's interest in Egypt. It had "rubbed off" on me and was the embryo that would eventually develop into my personal journey between souls.

I missed the 1972 Tutankhamun Exhibition at the British Museum, having been confined to a hospital bed, and had to settle for my mother's awe-filled accounts of it and my own "vision" of the golden mask of the boy king. I hoarded newspaper cuttings and posters on the topic. Although I did not envy the long lines of visitors their wait, I would have gladly done just the same. I vowed to research the ancient Egyptians upon my release from hospital and, when the time was right, I would travel to Egypt to see for myself all the wonders of that mystic land.

Eventually I plucked up the courage to write to Richard, inviting him to lecture in my area, but did not really expect to get a reply. I was in for a delightful surprise when a letter dated 27 June 1973 from an "R. Adamson" arrived:

"Thank you for your kind letter re the Tutankhamun lecture. I should be delighted to visit the Medway area in order to present the lecture which I have now given all over the country.

It has cost me a large amount to obtain my photos back from Egypt, together with two films (one made in 1923 and the other a television documentary). The insurance on these items and the 3500 years old necklace is enormous.

I would leave the date of the lecture to you but would suggest that you give two dates in case one is already booked."

When I had recovered enough from the shock of hearing from the man, I determined to go about finding a suitable venue for the lecture. At the time, my life was full of commitments and restrictions: my husband was a military man, we were living in army married quarters near Chatham in the south of England, and wherever I went I would invariably have my baby daughter Lisa in tow. However, I considered this new development a quest and visited the Chatham Town Hall to try my luck.

I parked Lisa's pushchair outside and headed for the information desk, clutching my letter from Richard close to my chest in an effort to "be heard." I was finally ushered into the office of the Publicity and Entertainment Officer Roland Jones and put my ideas to him. As Britain was still on the tail end of Tutmania, my proposal seemed a viable proposition. Roland promised to do what he could to get the lecture under way. Shortly afterwards, I received this letter of confirmation that a date had been agreed between Richard and the Central Hall, Chatham.

"Just a hurried note before I leave to go to a lecture in Devon. I have had a letter from Roland Jones, the entertainment officer at Chatham Town Hall, inviting me to lecture on September 29th.

This is quite convenient and I have sent a letter back to confirm the date. I shall look forward to meeting you on that date. The lecture will be at the Central Hall. Please excuse hasty note."

Several communiqués later, we had "lift-off." The event was confirmed for 29 September 1973. I was caught up in a mad whirl of activity, and my family thought I had inevitably and literally gone mad. But they humoured me and secretly hoped that I would soon grow out of it. When the posters and programmes arrived, I became both apprehensive and excited at the same time. I was finally going to meet the only man in the world with firsthand knowledge of the discovery of Tutankhamun's tomb.

Saturday 29 September finally arrived. When we entered Central Hall, it was packed to capacity. My family and I were seated in the front row. When Richard walked on stage, he had so much "presence." He introduced himself, directed a "thank you" towards me, then launched into his story. I immediately realised how very few people can touch your life in such a way as to change it forever.

I heard his words and the recording of the restored trumpets from the tomb, saw the slides he had on show and watched the film footage of the opening of the tomb. I was enthralled, as was the entire audience that night. Richard held us all spellbound. We were transported back in time, 3,000 years, yet it seemed just a moment ago.

After the lecture that evening, my family and I were introduced to Richard, and we talked for a long time. What impressed me most was his sense of humour and his down-to-earth approach to life. He may have been part of a unique historical event, but to Richard, "It was all in the line of duty."

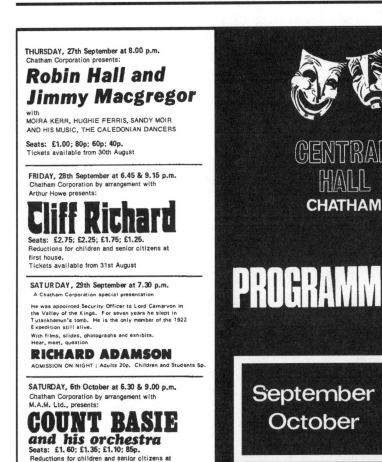

THURSDAY, 27th September at 8.00 p.m.
Chatham Corporation presents:

Robin Hall and Jimmy Macgregor

with
MOIRA KERR, HUGHIE FERRIS, SANDY MOIR
AND HIS MUSIC, THE CALEDONIAN DANCERS

Seats: £1.00; 80p; 60p; 40p.
Tickets available from 30th August

FRIDAY, 28th September at 6.45 & 9.15 p.m.
Chatham Corporation by arrangement with
Arthur Howe presents:

Cliff Richard

Seats: £2.75; £2.25; £1.75; £1.25.
Reductions for children and senior citizens at
first house.
Tickets available from 31st August

SATURDAY, 29th September at 7.30 p.m.
A Chatham Corporation special presentation

He was appointed Security Officer to Lord Carnarvon in
the Valley of the Kings. For seven years he slept in
Tutankhamun's tomb. He is the only member of the 1922
Expedition still alive.
With films, slides, photographs and exhibits.
Hear, meet, question

RICHARD ADAMSON

ADMISSION ON NIGHT : Adults 20p. Children and Students 5p.

SATURDAY, 6th October at 6.30 & 9.00 p.m.
Chatham Corporation by arrangement with
M.A.M. Ltd., presents:

COUNT BASIE
and his orchestra

Seats: £1.60; £1.35; £1.10; 85p.
Reductions for children and senior citizens at
first house.
Tickets available from 8th September.

CENTRAL HALL CHATHAM

PROGRAMME

September October

Roland Jones

On Saturday, 29 September 1973, I learned that if you open your mind enough, the past, present and future can come flooding in and enrich your very soul. I was a little bit further along the road.

* * * * * * *

9

REKINDLED
SPIRITS

Following the Central Hall lecture, I returned to my largely domestic existence, all the more energized by my obsession with Egypt. Richard continued to give lectures at schools, colleges, universities and private institutions, with people attending his lectures over and over again. He was totally committed and dedicated to his work and soon became something of a celebrity—touring, talking and meeting people from all walks of life.

We continued to correspond and saw each other from time to time. This gave me a chance to get to know the man a little better. He was modest in a flamboyant way. When people asked him what it was like to sleep in the tomb, he said, "It used to get boring sometimes, but that's what I was paid to do." He was quite blasé about it except during one point in his lectures. He used to become very animated when he talked about the moment he took his very first look in the tomb. Up to that point, he had thought, "These people are just muckin' about." When Carter made a hole in the sealed door to the antechamber, Richard began to change his tune. "At first, it was like seeing a heavy mist or fog and a lot of dust. There was a horrible smell. But then when it cleared, I could not believe my eyes." When Carter and his crew started bringing tomb objects out in the daylight, Richard realised, "This is quite a position to be in. I'm really part of something here."

From then on, Richard took a personal interest in the activities of the professionals at the site, "I was no archaeologist. I doubt if I could have even spelled the word, but Howard Carter drilled me in everything. I even helped with the unwrapping of the King's mummy. Carter and I were the only ones who stayed the whole 10 years."

After he left Egypt, Richard packed away his memories for many years. I learned that it wasn't until his early retirement from the Admiralty and the start of his lecture travels that it recurred to him that something really extraordinary had happened to him. It wasn't until he reflected and thought, "Oh, my God, I was part of that," or other people reminded him of it by asking, "What was it like?" that he stopped and remembered, "I was really there."

The making of a feature film was just the thing to keep Richard focussed and firmly fixed on the future. *The Curse of King Tutankhamen's Tomb*, a multi-million-pound fiction-founded-on-fact saga was based largely on Barry Wynne's book *Behind the Mask of Tutankhamen*, and the cast included many of Richard's favourite actors. Richard was recruited as a technical consultant during the early stages of the

The Curse of King Tutankhamen's Tomb

ROBIN ELLIS
EVA MARIE SAINT
HARRY ANDREWS
WENDY HILLER
ANGHARAD REES
TOM BAKER
with RAYMOND BURR

Drama based on Barry Wynne's book *Behind the Mask of Tutankhamen*.

In November, 1922, Howard Carter and his backer, Lord Carnarvon, made an extraordinary discovery in the Valley of the Kings, near Luxor, Egypt. He found a pharaoh's tomb.

But the rumour of an ancient curse, of impending grief and disaster, threatens to mar their triumph.

The narrator is Paul Scofield.

Howard Carter	Robin Ellis
Lord Carnarvon	Harry Andrews
Lady Evelyn Herbert	Angharad Rees
Princess Velma	Wendy Hiller
Sarah Morrissey	Eva Marie Saint
Jonash Sabastian	Raymond Burr
Lady Almina Carnarvon	Faith Brook
Hassan	Tom Baker
Collins	Rupert Frazer
Daoud	Stefan Kalipha
Amed Nahas	Darien Angadi
Fishbait	John Palmer
Lieutenant	Andy Pantelidou
Stallholder	Alfred Hoffman
Doctor	Rex Holdsworth

DIRECTOR PHILIP LEACOCK : PRODUCER PETER GRAHAM SCOTT : EXECUTIVE PRODUCER PATRICK DROMGOOLE *HTV Production*

HTV/Columbia Films

production and received a percentage of the first advances on royalties for his efforts.

Much of the filming was carried out in Egypt after Richard's involvement was complete, and it was here that "that damned curse" was blamed for delays and accidents that normally plague motion picture crews everywhere. But one specific event was enough to cause over 70 actors and technicians to quit the production and return immediately to Europe. During rehearsal in the desert mountains, actor Ian McShane (originally cast as Howard Carter) and actress Eva Marie Saint narrowly escaped death when their Model A Ford experienced brake failure and plunged over a 40-foot cliff. A shaken McShane soon left the production and was replaced by Robin Ellis.

Richard's semi-retirement also afforded an ideal opportunity for him to reflect on his life, where he had been and what he had done—old soldiers tend to do that. I learned how humble he felt at having been there in the right place at the right time—to have witnessed this incredible discovery firsthand. For a man not given easily to emotions, this was a rare insight into his mind.

His health deteriorated considerably over the next several years, but he continued to captivate his audiences and keep them roaring with laughter. The injuries he had suffered in World War I had by now taken their toll, and he was suffering immensely from them. Due to several factors (none of which had anything to do with an Egyptian curse), he had to have both his legs amputated at the hip. The operations were performed at The Queen Alexandra Hospital, Cosham, in Portsmouth.

Even after undergoing major surgery with such serious consequences, he managed to joke about his situation. On one occasion, he read a letter in the ward and announced,

"I've got that job as a bricklayer!" Nothing was going to keep him down for long, not even a double amputation. On 30 March 1980, Richard wrote:

"How nice to hear from you again. As you now know, I have had a long spell in hospital and finished up with both legs being amputated. I have recovered from the operations and am awaiting a transfer from this hospital to a permanent residence in an ex-servicemen's home in Surrey: The Royal Star & Garter Home.

I have already been there for an interview and am just awaiting the "documentation" (a favourite service expression) to be completed, and then I will be moving. The doctors would not consider me returning to my home as I live alone, and they thought it would be a risk.

I am, however, still continuing with the lectures. I have given two here at the hospital (on the night before the operation). The Sister of the ward nearly went mad when I told her I intended doing the lectures.

She tried to stop me, and the doctors did too, but I gave the lecture to all the staff, doctors, nurses and consultants, etc., and later I gave a second lecture, sitting in a wheelchair, with a nurse behind me.

I am continuing the university lectures also—I now have to travel by car, with my wheelchair in the boot. I quite like it. The last lecture I did was in my wheelchair seated on a dais, audience 300, and one at Portsmouth Guildhall, audience 1500."

The Royal Star & Garter Home started life as the once famous Star & Garter Hotel. During World War I, the British Red Cross was charged with the responsibility of establishing and managing a permanent home for disabled ex-servicemen on their discharge from military hospitals, and the old hotel was purchased for that purpose.

The home opened its doors to the first 65 patients in 1916, but the converted building was to prove totally unsuitable. Funds were eventually raised for 200 fully equipped rooms, wards and beds. On 10 July 1924, King George V and Queen Mary formally opened the building now known as the Royal Star & Garter Home for Disabled Soldiers, Sailors and Airmen.

The veterans of World War I have, through the years, been joined by the victims of World War II and by men who have since seen active service. Once Richard understood that he could no longer live on his own, he specifically requested the Royal Star & Garter Home so he could be with fellow ex-servicemen. His social life at the home helped smooth the transition from independence in his own Hampshire dwelling to managed care in a home for the disabled.

Once settled in the home, he endured a long and painful course of physiotherapy, yet was still determined to continue with the lectures. The staff encouraged him, believing that such an activity would do for his mind and intellect what the therapy was intended to do for his body.

In the two years following the amputations, Richard lectured to enthusiastic audiences at places such as the exclusive Roedean girls' school, Oxford University, the Egyptian Embassy, the London Festival Hall and—in Richard's words—"a private lecture here in London" (irrespective of the venue, his only demand was that his

Royal Star & Garter Home

Royal Star & Garter Home

*The Royal Star & Garter Home for
Disabled Soldiers, Sailors and Airmen*

basic costs were paid and that a donation be made to the Royal Star & Garter Home). The "private lecture" comment had the sound of mischief to it, so I quizzed him on the matter. The mystery was solved when he reluctantly offered the following:

> ". . . On July 29th I went to the Queen's royal garden party at Buckingham Palace. I met HRH Prince Charles, the Prince of Wales, and we had a long talk about the film and other matters. He knew I was here at the Royal Star & Garter Home and promised to look me up in a few weeks (which he did!) . . ."

In another correspondence, Richard wrote,

> ". . . Since I have been here we have had 'outings' to the Royal Chelsea Flower Show, Kew Gardens, the Trooping of the Colours on Horseguards Parade and a trip to Margate . . ."

It was good to hear that he was enjoying life, but it was his next remark that nearly threw me off my chair,

> ". . . I now go horse-riding every Friday. Instruction by the London Mounted Police. They were all astounded here when I first asked, but the doc said, 'why not!' and approved my application."

Life at the Royal Star & Garter Home was not without the occasional "big event." H.R.H. Princess Alexandra made a formal visit to the home in late 1980. Having recently toured Egypt and the Valley of the Kings, she spent considerable time talking with Richard about the Tutankhamun tomb and its discovery.

During the course of Richard's transition to the Royal Star & Garter Home, my husband had concluded his service career and we had migrated to his birthplace known as the

Royal Star & Garter Home

*Princess Alexandra talking to
Richard Adamson at the
Royal Star & Garter Home, 1980*

"Lake District" in the north-west of England. We were living in a town called Millom, and I was once again juggling a full-time job with raising a family. My husband was now a police officer, working incredibly varied hours.

To keep Richard ticking along after the huge changes in his lifestyle, I invited him to my new home in one of Britain's most beautiful areas. He gladly accepted the invitation and agreed to give a lecture during his stay.

Using the techniques that had proven successful in Chatham, I managed to hire the local Millom Palladium for £50. Local enthusiasts and my family worked together to arrange the finer details. We had a whale of a time arranging the affair and were ecstatic when all tickets were sold in advance. The venue proved to be an excellent choice. Since Millom Palladium is more used to accommodating the local amateur operatic society than presenting lectures on ancient Egypt, it caused quite a stir in early October 1980 when a billboard reading "An Evening with Richard Adamson" was installed over the entrance.

Sister June Bailey was Richard's escort for the trip to Millom. Special ramps had been ordered for his wheelchair, and British Rail removed a seat in the carriage to accommodate it. True, the long journey was tiring for him, but Sister Bailey made sure he was well looked after, and he was cheerful and raring to go as soon as he settled into his "quarters" at Brockwood Park in the Whicham Valley, a few miles outside Millom. This proved to be an excellent location for him to relax and enjoy his surroundings.

I thought it impossible that his wheelchair would ever fit through our cottage doorway, even after taking the front door off. We also had narrow twisting stairways and corridors, and huge front steps to negotiate. All that fuss would have normally made Richard feel uncomfortable. He did it, though. He insisted on seeing our humble home. It helped him fix in his mind where we were, and he needed to do that, he told us. He loved our company, the questions and eager faces of my children excited by it all. My youngest daughter had made him a sheepskin case for his spectacles. He treasured it, keeping it always in his inside pocket.

After dinner on the evening of Friday, 3 October 1980, Richard gave the Brockwood Park hosts a private presentation, staying up until the early hours of the morning. Despite his age and disability, he was never still for a moment during his visit to Millom. He enjoyed the local interest and special treatment bestowed upon him.

As the lecture was not until 7:30 pm the next day, we had arranged to take Richard and Sister Bailey out into the glorious countryside with its spectacular mountains and lakes. They saw it at its best, in all its autumn glory, bedecked in reds and golds, "second only to the beauty of that golden mask," Richard was to say later.

I found myself having difficulty keeping up with him at times. I seemed destined to always be "recovering from something or other" whenever I needed extra strength. On this occasion, I had needed an emergency operation and was still in the process of recovering. When I looked at Richard and saw the way he was holding up, all thoughts of how I was going to cope soon vanished.

I stood before a full house Saturday evening and introduced Richard to the people of Cumbria—and Lancashire, Northumbria, Yorkshire, Scotland and places even further afield. Richard directed operations from his chair with precision and, as usual, kept everyone laughing at the right moments. Because I knew him fairly well by this time, I was aware that at times he was in excruciating pain during his performance, but he never revealed his suffering to his audiences.

What was so impressive on that evening was the rapt attention of the little ones, my own included, who sat enthralled. Not a snack in sight, no fidgeting, just a sort of hushed reverence for this man and his "tales from the tomb." The local press photographer Neville Robson worked hard that night, and the scramble for autographs was impressive as young and old alike took their turn in the queue.

Richard was exhausted when he finished his presentation, so we drove him back to Brockwood Park as soon as possible. The next day, we took him out for one last look at Lakeland. He did not usually have time to see much of the places he visited, as he was so busy travelling from one venue to another. He read up on the sites, but usually had time for just a cursory glance as he made his way from one function to another. This time, though, we were determined that he get as much out of his visit as possible.

Simon Edgar

Neville Robson

*Richard Adamson signing autographs
after the 1980 Millom lecture*

He was obviously impressed with his stay, as revealed in
this note that he penned on his return to Richmond:

> "Thank you all for your most kind hospitality.
> I will not forget my visit to Cumbria—it will
> always remain with me. You all worked so hard,
> and Sister Bailey has been talking about it ever
> since. I did not know that she was actually on
> holiday when she was asked to escort me to
> Millom. She came straight back and has now

Neville Robson

*Adamson with
author Elaine Edgar*

resumed her holiday, but told me, 'I am going back there. It is a wonderful place!' Many thanks for a wonderful weekend. All my love, Richard."

As I read that note, my thoughts at first echoed his words, "Many thanks for a wonderful weekend." Then as my mind wandered back to Richard's past and the great Egyptian adventure, his words mingled with those that Howard Carter had used over half a century before. I found myself repeating:

A wonderful weekend, a wonderful weekend.
. . . a wonderful day . . . wonderful things . . .

* * * * * * * *

10

THE LAST SURVIVOR

Richard's last big adventure was his return to Egypt in 1981 after a period of nearly 60 years. He was by then an octogenarian.

Aramco World magazine and their regular contributing writer John Lawton were Richard's main sources of encouragement. Lawton, inspired by a local newspaper article on Richard's exploits in Egypt, visited Richard at the Royal Star & Garter Home to find out more. If the story proved to be credible, Lawton intended to approach his editor Robert Arndt with the idea to take Richard on a nostalgic visit back to the tomb.

> "I was astounded—and skeptical. Particularly when a perusal of several Tutankhamen books— including Carter's definitive work—showed no

trace of any 'Adamson.' He was not mentioned in any index. There was not a single photograph . . ." [1]

This was, of course, because Richard had been, through necessity as well as requirement, a "silent witness" when the history books were being written. His silence was finally broken upon his retirement and the start of his lecture tours.

John Lawton was impressed after listening to Richard's own account of his time in the Valley of the Kings, of being the guest of Prince Charles at Trinity College, Cambridge, and giving over 1,500 lectures on the topic. Then there was Richard's lecture suitcase, crammed full with letters, photographs, press cuttings and other documentation—a treasure trove in itself. But most of all, it was Richard himself who convinced Lawton of his authenticity.

Aramco World agreed to fund the project, and permission was soon obtained from the Royal Star & Garter Home. Richard could not wait to get started. He was to be escorted by his Irish nurse (Mary Lally), John Lawton and photographer Tor Eigeland.

There were real challenges and hazards to overcome on such a long trip in a relatively undeveloped land. Richard was a diabetic and had lost both legs—he was thus wheelchair-bound. As 1981 was the United Nation's International Year of Disabled Persons, it was hoped to demonstrate that disability does not automatically bar the determined from making even the most difficult of journeys.

Richard and his companions finally set off for Egypt, but this journey was to be very different from Richard's previous one. It started with a comfortable five-hour British Airways

---

1. Photographs and quotations regarding Richard Adamson's 1981 visit to Egypt by kind permission of *Aramco World.*

flight from London to Cairo, on which he was pampered all the way by airline staff and attended by his personal nurse.

> ". . . Driving into Cairo from the airport, Adamson said it seemed like only yesterday that he had patrolled the city's streets. He easily picked out landmarks, even in the dark, reeled off street names like a Cairo taxi driver, and regaled us with his exploits as a young military policeman sixty years before . . ."

In Cairo, he was given almost V.I.P. treatment by the Hilton Hotel and a large, comfortable room complete with fruit, flowers and a balcony view of the River Nile. He enjoyed gazing at the Nile, remembering tales of "Hapi" and recalling his years in Egypt. More importantly, Richard was reacquainted with his old tomb companions—the Ka statues—and other treasures from the tomb, on display in the Cairo Museum.

In 1922, he had travelled from Cairo to Luxor by train. This time it was but a short EgyptAir flight and an extremely uneventful journey until a group of enthusiastic Egyptians grabbed the wheelchair then hoisted man and machine over a parked car that blocked their path. "That would not have happened in England," a startled Richard yelped. Although Egypt had none of the special facilities that disabled people in the West have become accustomed to, there were always plenty of willing hands to assist.

Even so, the occasional awkward moment occurred. On his arrival at the Winter Palace Hotel, Richard was forced to use the freight elevator rather than negotiate the grand stone staircase leading up to the famous building. But to Richard, the inelegance of such an entrance was nothing. When he had first arrived at the hotel in 1922, the sight of his grimy uniform and battered kit bag had caused the hotel

Aramco World-Tor Eigeland

(above)
Richard Adamson
looks out over Cairo
once again . . .
and (right) talks with
an Egyptian child

Aramco World-Tor Eigeland

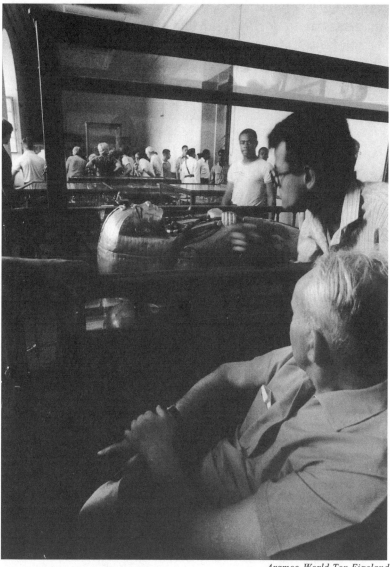

Aramco World-Tor Eigeland

*Re-viewing the inner coffin,
this time at the Cairo Museum*

staff to quickly whisk him into a room at the back to avoid embarrassment. In 1981, however, it was Richard who had the celebrity suite overlooking the Nile, to the envy of the other guests—the "package tourists."

Richard felt a surge of nostalgia as he surveyed the familiar hotel interior, still adorned with marble corridors and oriental carpets. The only changes he could detect were the absence of the lounge billiard table and of the whirring ceiling fans which had been replaced by air-conditioning.

The method of reaching the Valley of the Kings had remained basically the same, although a swarm of taxis had replaced the waiting donkeys for the overland portion of the trip. Crossing the Nile, however, was still achieved by ferry but with a few variations for a man in a wheelchair. John Lawton recalled:

> ". . . We avoided the wooden catwalk, for example, by sliding Adamson down the steep sandy bank to the water's edge, myself and two others acting as human brakes. After much argument with the boatman who wanted to put Richard on the open bow, we managed to get him safely inside. Unfortunately, getting out the other side of the ferry on the west bank of the river proved impossible— until someone wrenched the sliding cabin door right off its rollers, giving us just enough room to squeeze Adamson and his wheelchair through.
>
> The tremendous crash brought an irate boatman running, and we had to pay for the door to calm him. Then we carried Adamson up the steps from the quay and, at the top, ran a gauntlet of taxi-drivers, each trying to pull the wheelchair towards his own taxi. I resolved the contest by selecting a minibus, and we drove away leaving the drivers scuffling as a policeman tried to restore order . . ."

The minibus took the party directly into the Valley of the Kings. Richard was by now, of course, a rather "old soldier," and memories of his youth were sweet. He was allowed to visit the tomb on his own, without any tourists present. As the small party moved towards the 16 steps, Lawton the journalist reverted to type and began to think about the curse:

> ". . . as we struggled to get Adamson and his wheelchair down the steps to Tut's tomb, I couldn't help thinking it was an ideal time for the pharaoh to strike again. The steps and the passageway plunge at a 45-degree angle into the earth and with only two of us able to get a proper grip on the chair, one slip that day and Adamson could have hurtled down the whole flight . . ."

When Richard was inevitably asked if the loss of his legs could have been a result of the curse, he reassured his host, "I lost them through the curse of war and no other curse."

Lawton observed that Richard was visibly moved by the experience of returning to the place of his exile:

> ". . . At first, he was confused by the changes made in the meantime—the dividing wall between the antechamber and burial chamber has been removed and replaced by a railed platform—but soon got his bearings. 'Right there,' he said, pointing to the space between the giant quartzite sarcophagus and the wall of the burial chamber, 'that's where I had my bed.' And for a few moments he sat there in the narrow passage, lost in thought, his head bowed, his eyes half closed and saying nothing . . ."

In the meantime, crowds of tourists had formed above ground and were angrily protesting at being kept waiting. As a result, Richard Adamson, the last survivor of the

Aramco World-Tor Eigeland

*Richard Adamson, with Nurse Lally following,
descends once more into Tutankhamun's tomb*

discovery, was allowed less than five minutes to recall all the memories of that time long ago. But he did not complain. On reaching the surface again, Richard said to Lawton, "I never dreamed that I would ever come back again for even such a brief visit. Thank you very much for bringing me."

During his visit, Richard remained mischieviously cheerful and not at all self-conscious of his immobility. At airports, he amused his companions by asking startled shoe-shine boys to polish his boots. In the air, he would demand "a pair of in-flight slippers, like everyone else" from perplexed airline cabin staff. Only once did he display annoyance: when ground staff at Cairo airport attempted to place him on a stretcher to carry him off the plane, he barked, "I don't need that damn thing yet!"

* * * * * * * *

Upon his return from Egypt, Richard continued to give talks and lectures, but these became increasingly infrequent. The trip had exhausted him, although he never admitted it, and his health gradually deteriorated over the months that followed.

He was delighted when *Aramco World* published an article "The Last Survivor" at the end of 1981. The nine-page piece was lavishly illustrated and gave a detailed account of his return to Egypt and the Valley of the Kings. It had been a unique sentimental journey for Richard, and even in his weakened state he gave thanks that, at last, the purveyors of print had got it right.

In July 1982, Richard's eldest surviving son, Edward Adamson, received a telephone call from the Royal Star & Garter Home. Edward's father was extremely ill and was not expected to last more than 72 hours. Edward immediately made the two-hour journey to London. Three times Richard

Photographer unknown

(l-r) Agnes Knight and June Bailey (Richard's "minders"), Richard Adamson, author Elaine Edgar

rallied after being pronounced dead but finally, in the early hours of 18 July, Richard Adamson's eventful life ended.

June Bailey, by then Matron of the Royal Star & Garter Home, telephoned me with news of Richard's death at the age of 81. I was devastated but not entirely surprised as he had been suffering immensely. In a way his passing was a happy release, but I had lost a dear friend and mentor, and the world had lost the last member of the Tutankhamun discovery expedition.

Never again would his words be heard echoing through the halls and universities of England. His humour would no longer relate to all the different generations of people who had crowded to hear him speak. I retain the fondest memories of him to this day—that smiling face, his wicked grin, his special presence.

Chris Wood

* * * * * * * *

11

A JOURNEY BETWEEN SOULS

I continued to keep in touch with the Royal Star & Garter Home and wrote regularly to Matron June Bailey. She had been one of my many links to Richard, and we became good friends over the years.

From time to time, I came across something that reminded me of him, and it saddened me to think that he was gone. I never seemed to get around to collating the many letters, pictures, press cuttings and other things he had given me over the years. I often felt guilty that I had not found the time to arrange the scraps of evidence of Richard Adamson's remarkable story and, to use his words, "get it all down on paper" as he had encouraged me to do so many times. It was just too painful to contemplate the memories and the task. Instead, I made countless excuses for not starting the enormous research project that would be required. I had four lively children to raise, a full-time career and charity work. Yet part of Richard remained in my soul—and my soul kept crying "Egypt."

For eight years after Richard's death I battled with these emotions. Then, in 1990, I had finally saved enough money for a visit to Egypt—Cairo, Luxor and the Valley of the Kings. I had so many preconceived ideas of what to expect that I could almost "smell" the essence of the place before I set foot upon its soil. But I was determined that it would be the trip of a lifetime!

I made the journey with my mother and my sister Tricia. We had booked our trip with Bales Tours, a leading UK tour operator for exclusive holidays. Their special groups manager, Anthony Bales, provided us with such a potpourri of expertise that for eight days we were subjected to nothing less than wonderment. We also had the services of an excellent local guide—Mohamed Gamal el din Montisir.

Despite the descriptions Richard had fed me and all the photographs I had seen, I was completely taken aback by the ruins of the ancient monuments which had retained their dignity despite centuries of neglect and annual bombardments by sand and sightseers. My mother and Tricia felt the same way—we had all found paradise. The single disappointment was that my star attraction—Tutankhamun's tomb—was closed.

Convinced that my odyssey was not yet complete, I contacted Anthony Bales again. Together we arranged a "special group" visit for the following year. I provided the proposed itinerary and Anthony plied his skills to make it happen. All I had to do in the meantime was recruit enough people to validate the word "group." Several work colleagues, some close friends and a few relations joined me on my second journey to Egypt. Mohamed Gamal was again our

*Mohamed Gamal el din
Montisir, on duty near the
stepped pyramid of Saqqara*

P. North

guide, and I once more experienced a sense of awe in that great land. Yet Pharaoh Tutankhamun continued to elude me, his tomb having been recently closed and locked by not-so-pious hands.

By 1993, I was adamant that "Richard's tomb" would not escape me much longer and vowed to return to Egypt as many times as necessary, until those 16 stone steps could lead me to the place where Richard had slept alone for so many nights. My sister Tricia and her husband Phil North accompanied me on my 1993 voyage. They proved invaluable as I was almost immediately confined to my cabin with a characteristic ailment, popularly known to tourists as "pharaoh's revenge."

Harry Hicks

Entrance to the Cairo Museum

Harry Hicks

Interior gallery of the Cairo Museum

I had to succumb to the ministrations of Dr. Baha Demian and his syringe rehydration technique before I was able to move around the deck with confidence. The doctor's peculiar prescription soon took effect, but even his expertise could not cure me in time to visit that special tomb in that special valley. The doctor and I have remained good friends to this day, despite his drastic measures. He has managed to keep me well enough to function properly on my subsequent visits to his country.

As a result of those first exploratory trips to Egypt, I became seriously interested in Egyptology. Although my hectic lifestyle left little space for new avenues of study, I managed to take a correspondence course given by Suzanne Bojtos of the Petrie Museum of Egyptian Archaeology. The knowledge gleaned from these studies enabled me to appreciate much more of what I witnessed on my journeys. I am sure that Richard would have been proud of me for investing the time in Egyptology, yet my thirst to walk in his footsteps above and below the Theban Hills remained unquenched.

Sometime during that course of study, my nephew Greg made a chance remark to his mother. He was describing that day's "Egyptian project session" in which a girl named Sarah Adamson had stood up and told the class about her great-grandfather who had been a security officer in the Valley of the Kings when the tomb of Tutankhamun was discovered. Tricia contacted me immediately with the news. The surname "Adamson" was all it took. With Tricia's help, I was soon in contact with the schoolteacher, a Mr. Buxton, and Sarah Adamson's parents. It is a scenario more befitting a fairy tale than the biography of a British soldier, but it is the truth: Richard Adamson's great-granddaughter Sarah and my nephew Greg North were attending the same school and working on a project about ancient Egypt.

I soon received a phone call from Sarah's father, Kevin Adamson (Richard's grandson), and we arranged to meet. I vividly remember the first time I visited Kevin, his wife Jane and their two children, Sarah and Richard jr. The resemblance between Kevin and Richard was staggering—it indeed evoked an "uncanny feeling" in me.

Kevin recalled . . .

"I remember him as a grandfather figure, always laughing and joking around, just taking care of the kids. He was a happy fellow, always happy. He was always all right. If you ever asked him how he was, he'd say, 'Oh, I'm fine,' even if he wasn't.

There was a period of time when he first came back from Egypt when all the information and photos and everything was locked away for years and years. It wasn't really spoken about. He had young children at the time, so he stuck it all in a box, put it up on a shelf, and it was forgotten.

I spent time with him through the '70s. When I was 14 or 15, I started to appreciate the Tutankhamun memorabilia he had. Later, I'd take him to different lectures, basically to give him a lift and save him the taxi fare. I'd set up his projector. Sometimes I'd stay and listen while the lecture was going on, and I got more and more interested. He was committed 100 percent to lecturing. He loved it. He always wore a suit when he lectured.

People would often ask him what he thought about Lord Carnarvon seeking advice from a palm reader—clairvoyants and the curse. He'd say, 'Well, that is what happened, but it's a load of rubbish.' He used to always say, 'No more rubbish! No more rubbish!'

Kevin Adamson

Kevin Adamson and family (daughter Sarah, wife Jane and son Richard jr.)

In 1982, I went up to London and visited him for the day, spent an hour or two with him. I knew then he probably wouldn't be around much longer because he said to me, 'I'm getting pretty fed up with all this now. I'm not happy with anything.' He was pretty easy going all his life, but now he said, 'I don't particularly like it anywhere at the moment.' That was the last time I saw him."

Kevin's father, Edward Adamson, confirmed his son's assessment of Richard Adamson's state of mind at the end of his life:

"He had always wanted to go back to Egypt. 'If there is something I'd wish in life it's to go back to the site, but there is no way I will do that now,' he told me. Then of course it materialised. After the trip to Egypt, he seemed to lose interest in life. I don't know why. He never talked about it. The way I see it is he had done what he wanted to do and he gave up. Quite possibly it's the way he wanted to go."

Kevin and I began piecing together our individual memories of his grandfather. When I told Kevin that his grandfather had frequently urged me to document his Tutankhamun story, he pledged his support and offered to encourage other members of the extended Adamson family to endorse the project. It was at that time that I vowed to honour Richard's request.

In December 1994, fate stepped in once more. During that year's attempt to gain access to the tomb of Tutankhamun, I had met Jill and Ron Slaughter—tourists on one of Bales' Egyptian tours. We enjoyed each other's company immensely and soon found that we had all married on the same day of the same year. We had plenty of time to talk about our lives and interests, and found we had much more in common, including a passionate interest in history and literature. On New Year's Eve of that visit, with my new-found friends, I finally walked down the 16 steps and into the tomb of Tutankhamun.

As I ventured through the empty antechamber and into the small stone-walled sanctuary that still houses the quartzite sarcophagus, my thoughts were strongly focussed on Richard. My journey between souls was complete in so many ways. I had at last joined him in his place of exile, had closed the circle of kinship with his family and now knew that I would somehow find the strength to complete his memoirs.

I have gained so much through my love of Egypt—and it has all evolved, in some way, through knowing Richard. In 1995 I celebrated my 30th wedding anniversary with my husband Royce, and Jill and Ron Slaughter. It was through them that I was introduced to the world of publishing, and the vision of Richard's book became a reality.

An undertaking such as this involves an enormous amount of planning, research and sleuthing. Kevin and Jane Adamson have worked exhaustingly with me on this project, and it is largely thanks to them that I had managed to piece together most of the jigsaw puzzle. But one important element continually eluded us throughout our quest: What had happened to Richard's battered old suitcase and its contents?

Kevin Adamson finally tracked down the suitcase filled with Richard's lecture notes, photographs, reports, cine film, 35-mm slides and other memorabilia. It had taken me 13 years to trace it, countless searches, detailed communications and diligent detective work before it finally surrendered itself from a dusty

Colin White

The battered suitcase that Richard Adamson carried around the lecture halls

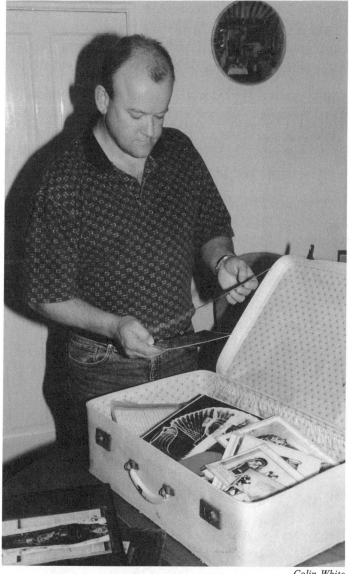

Colin White

Kevin Adamson examining
the suitcase contents shortly
after its discovery

old attic in Scotland, just across the border from Cumbria and the Lake District—practically on my doorstep. With this emotional and purposeful find, I felt even more inspired and able to comply with Richard's desire to commit his story to ink.

Thus I started on this work in earnest. I revisited old friends and acquaintances, bashed and bullied every lead I could find for association, confirmation and affirmation, until all sources were exhausted. As part of my quest, I journeyed to Highclere Castle (the Carnarvon family estate) and to the British Museum.

I considered the visit to Highclere a compulsory port-of-call, and an opportunity to say some kind of farewell to the fifth Earl on Richard's behalf. I lingered in the "Egyptian room" and discussed the reason for my interest with the attendant there. As I was about to leave the estate, I was introduced to the seventh Earl of Carnarvon, grandson of the man who financed

Highclere estate

The seventh Earl of Carnarvon

the great discovery. Lord Carnarvon has since provided support and encouragement by putting his staff at my disposal for research purposes.

At the British Museum, the necklace of Queen Hatshepsut that Richard had used to great effect in his lectures was not on public display, and there was some concern as to its whereabouts. I knew that it had been returned to the museum so I persevered. Fortunately a few enquiries and explanations took me to the inner sanctum of the museum where the precious item had been located and was made available for me to study.

Jill Slaughter, reproduced by permission of the British Museum

John Hayman of the British Museum and the author studying Queen Hatshepsut's necklace (ref: EA 74181)

The full honour Richard Adamson has deserved for so long can finally be paid to him. He spent much of his long life in anonymity, then in his later years finally received audience adulation and media attention. But in the end, this story, if nothing else, is a tribute to a great but unassuming man, to his courage and determination.

Richard, I feel privileged to have known you.

P. North

Some people come into our lives and quickly go.
Some stay for a while, touch our hearts, and we are
never, ever, the same.[1]

Flavia Weedn

* * * * * * * *

---

appendix 1

A CONCISE HISTORY

The period portrayed in this book concerning the life and times of Richard Adamson spans almost a century. If one adds the events of antiquity resulting in the construction and furnishing of the tomb of Tutankhamun, we have a time frame that encompasses thousands of years. This appendix serves to document the chronology of the days of Pharaoh Tutankhamun, his tomb and of Richard Adamson's life.

Precise dates prescribed to events of antiquity are the subject of much debate and disagreement within the worlds of ancient history and Egyptian archaeology. The dates suggested here are derived from *Atlas of Ancient Egypt* by John Baines and Jaromir Malek.

1323 BC	Death of Pharaoh Tutankhamun. Body entombed in the Valley of the Kings.
1319 BC	First robbery of Tutankhamun's tomb. Second robbery of tomb, resulting in Royal Necropolis officials repairing breach holes and resealing annexe, antechamber and tomb entrance.
1151-1143 BC	Tomb of Rameses VI started. Workmen's huts constructed over the buried entrance to Tutankhamun's tomb.
1000 BC	Royal Necropolis at Thebes dismantled. King Tutankhamun's tomb missed during this activity.
1798	Napoleon Bonaparte conquers Egypt. French soldier discovers Rosetta stone, allowing hieroglyphs to be deciphered for the first time.
1891	Howard Carter arrives in Egypt.
1901	Richard Adamson born.
1902	Theodore Davis granted concession to excavate in the Valley of the Kings.
1914	Lord Carnarvon awarded concession to dig in the Valley of the Kings. Start of World War I.
1918	End of World War I. Carnarvon expedition resumed.
1919	Richard Adamson posted to Cairo, Egypt; also serves in Jerusalem.
1922	Richard Adamson posted to Luxor/ Valley of the Kings.

Discovery of the first step leading to the tomb of Tutankhamun.
Howard Carter and Lord Carnarvon gain access to antechamber and annexe.
Access to burial chamber and treasury.
Official opening antechamber/annexe.
First object removed from tomb.

1923	Lord Carnarvon signs contract with *The Times* newspaper. Opening of the burial chamber. Death of Lord Carnarvon. First objects delivered to Cairo Museum.
1924	Lifting of sarcophagus lid. The 'strike' and lock-out. Howard Carter leaves for U.S.A. tour. Richard Adamson takes first leave of absence and marries.
1925	New concession to continue work. Burial shrine dismantled and mummy revealed. Start of autopsy on mummy.
1926	Start of work on treasury.
1927	Start of work on annexe.
1928	Death of Arthur C. Mace.
1930	Final objects removed from tomb.
1932	Final objects shipped to Cairo. Richard Adamson returns to England.
1939	Death of Howard Carter. Start of World War II. Richard Adamson enlists in R.A.F. Volunteer Reserve.

1940	Battle of Britain. Death of Harry Burton.
1967	Death of Kate Adamson.
1968	Second autopsy of Tutankhamun. Richard Adamson begins lecturing in U.K.
1972	Tutankhamun exhibition at the British Museum, London.
1978, 1980	Richard Adamson's legs amputated.
1981	Richard Adamson revisits Cairo, the Valley of the Kings and Pharaoh Tutankhamun's tomb.
1982	Death of Richard Adamson.
1995	Richard Adamson's lecture suitcase discovered in attic in Scotland.

* * * * * * * *

appendix 2

TOMB TREASURES

This appendix gives an overview of the range of artefacts found in the tomb of Tutankhamun. Most of the treasures are in the possession of the Cairo Museum where a wide selection remains on permanent display.

archery equipment
baskets
beds
bier
boat models
boomerangs and throw-sticks
botanical specimens
boxes
chests
canopic equipment
chairs, stools
chariots

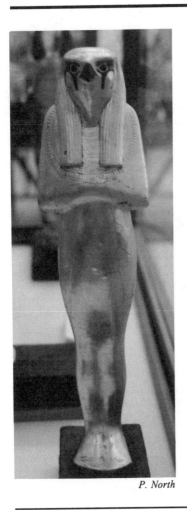

P. North

(above) gold statue and
(previous page) golden throne,
as currently displayed in the
Cairo Museum

clothing
coffins
cosmetic articles
cuirass
divine figures
fans
foodstuff
gaming equipment
gold mask
granary model
hassocks
jewellery, beads, amulets
labels
lamps and torches
mummies
musical instruments
pall and framework
pavillion
regalia
ritual couches
ritual objects
royal figures and figurines
sarcophagus
seals
shabtis
shrines
sticks, staves
swords, daggers, shields
tools
vessels
wine jars
writing equipment

* * * * * * * *

appendix 3

SUITCASE TREASURES

The "aging, battered suitcase" belonging to Richard Adamson and discovered in an attic in Scotland in 1995 (see Chapter 11) was filled to capacity with memorabilia relating to the Tutankhamun discovery. Although of little material value, it reflects a lifetime of dedication to an honourable cause: the preservation of historical fact.

The suitcase contained two binders, one packed with discoloured prints of some of Harry Burton's justly famous photographs, and the other crammed with a miscellany of photocopied and typed original documents relating to the discovery. Also present was a collection of enlargements of some of the photographs (crudely mounted on boards), a set of 35-mm colour slides used in Adamson's lectures, and two short reels of 8-mm black-and-white cine film (including original footage of the tomb opening).

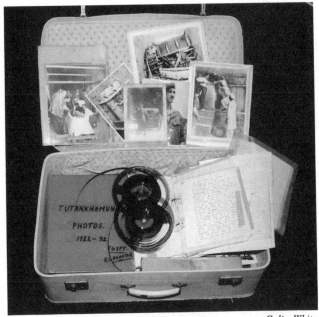

Colin White

Overview of the suitcase contents

Colin White

(left) one of Harry Burton's photographs;
(right) part of Mervyn Herbert's journal;
(center) cine films

A small set of professionally produced copy negatives of some of Harry Burton's photographs was found tucked behind the material at the back of the suitcase, and the reason for their presence remains a mystery. No other hidden compartments, sewn-in pockets or secret stowings, nor any indications of clandestine activities regarding Egyptian relics were found.

The document binder is by far the most interesting item. It contains personal documents and other materials both entrusted and donated to Adamson by others for his personal enjoyment, and these have proved invaluable in the preparation of this book The most significant of these are:

■ A range of pages photocopied from the original handwritten 1922/23 journal of the Hon. Mervyn Herbert. The verbatim quotations in Chapters 3 and 4 were extracted from these pages, thanks to the kind permission of The Executors of Mervyn Herbert.

■ Richard's account of the Cairo Conspiracy Trial (included in Chapter 1).

■ Press cuttings from a wide selection of newspaper articles and reviews from the many U.K. lectures.

■ Most importantly, a set of typewritten pages that describe the discovery of the tomb of Tutankhamun.

This latter document or "script" constituted the main element of Richard Adamson's lectures and was compiled largely from field notes, reports and other writings that Richard typed for Howard Carter and others at the discovery site during the period 1922-1925. The following transcript of the lecture script continues from the text included in Chapter 3. Much of the text of this portion subsequently appeared in *The Tomb of Tut-ankh-Amen* by Howard Carter and A.C. Mace, albeit in refined and embellished form.

AN ARCHAEOLOGICAL ADVENTURE

THE DISCOVERY OF
TUT-ANKH-AMUN'S TOMB.
EGYPT, NOVEMBER 1922.

by Richard Adamson

During 1922, I was present in Egypt as a member of the Military Police when I was sent to the "Valley of the Kings" to look after the property of Lord Carnarvon and Howard Carter who were about to finish excavating as the concession they held was due to terminate.

On November 3rd, 1922, I was watching the workmen uncovering some ancient huts used during the building of the tomb of Rameses VI and noticed one large stone somewhat different from the rest. The workmen at once began to cover this up again, but I took some photos of the stone and position.

The workmen then began to dig away from this stone to a different area.

When Howard Carter arrived the following morning, I mentioned this to him and, as the photos had by then been developed and printed, we were able to pinpoint the spot. The stone was uncovered once more and proved to be the first of a flight of steps leading down into the hillside.

At the time, I was not clear as to why the workmen had tried to hide this stone, but later events gave the explanation.

(At one period, the Egyptian Government withdrew the extended concession and placed their own officials in charge, with disastrous results to the preservation of the treasures. After prolonged negotiations, Howard Carter was recalled and again took charge.)

It would appear that, had the tomb NOT been discovered on the morning of the 4th of November 1922, the concession—about to end—would not have been renewed. The Egyptians would then have recommenced excavations on the site of the original stone step—they had guessed what it was—and the Lord Carnarvon-Howard Carter expedition could never have claimed the discovery of the tomb.

After the flight of steps had been uncovered, a sealed doorway was found at the bottom which showed signs of having been opened and sealed up again. This door was removed to reveal a long passage filled with rubble and chippings. It was some thirty feet long. This was cleared to reveal another sealed doorway, again with the signs of having been opened and resealed.

Before removing this door, Howard Carter made a test to determine the nature of the air on the other side. He made a small hole in the top left-hand corner and inserted a lighted candle.

We stood and watched as the flame flickered for a moment and then became a steady flame. Howard Carter then looked inside.

The silence was intense until Lord Carnarvon broke the silence and called out, "Can you see anything, Carter?" "Yes," was the reply, "Wonderful things, wonderful things." He stepped down and then Lord Carnarvon, who had by then been handed a torch, stepped up and looked. His face was almost white as he stepped down and the others took their turn to look. Eventually the torch was handed to me and I stepped up and looked inside.

I do not know what I expected to see, but most certainly the sight took my breath away. As I moved the torch around, details of the vault emerged. It appeared to be full of objects the like of which no man had ever seen or was likely to see again.

I quote from the notes Howard Carter sent to the Cairo Museum at the time: "I suppose most excavators would confess to a feeling of awe when they break into a chamber closed and sealed by pious hands so many centuries ago. For the moment, time as a factor in human life has lost its meaning. Three thousand, four thousand years maybe have passed and gone since human feet last trod the floor on which you stand and yet, as you note the signs of recent life around you, the half-filled bowl of mortar for the door, the blackened lamp, the finger mark upon the freshly painted surface, the farewell garland dropped upon the threshold—you feel it might have been but yesterday. The very air you breathe, unchanged throughout the centuries, you share with those who laid the mummy to its rest. Time is annihilated by little intimate details such as these, and you feel an intruder."

As I looked into the vault, what most attracted attention were three huge couches in the form of animals, uncanny and grotesque, covered in gold. My gaze kept constantly returning to these objects as if drawn to them by a magnet. All around in utter profusion were chests, vases, shrines (from the open doors of one peered the head of a snake), boxes, chariots, thrones, chairs, miniature statues and everywhere, the glint of gold. The mind would not register what the eye could see. At the other end of the vault were two life-sized statues in black, overlaid in gold, facing each other like sentinels, gold-kilted, gold-sandalled, carrying mace and staff, upon their foreheads the royal emblems of the sacred Cobra and Vulture.

We could, however, see no mummy and then we noticed that between the two statues was another sealed doorway. The explanation could only mean that this was only the threshold of the discovery, that behind that door would be found another chamber even more wonderful than that which we were now looking at and, in that chamber, in all the magnificent panoply of death would be found the Pharaoh.

The next day the tomb was entered and as I stood inside and again looked at the two statues guarding the sealed doorway, one had the feeling that perhaps we were not intended to have ever seen what we were now looking at, that the Priests who had closed this tomb had hoped that it would remain inviolate forever. It was an uncanny feeling, as if we were in the presence of someone who, although dead, was still alive and watching. You seemed to inherit almost at once the belief of those long dead Egyptians that they do not die but live on again in the spirit of their Gods.

As I stood there surrounded by the everyday articles of a long dead Pharaoh, I could almost picture the scenes of that life. I looked at a golden drinking cup containing a sediment which was later found to be wine. In one corner was a bouquet of flowers still in position as they had been placed over three thousand years before. It appeared as if it was only yesterday.

Any object would have satisfied any archaeologist as a treasure, yet here were hundreds of such objects.

Howard Carter decided to clear this first or Antechamber before opening the sealed door by the two statues, and each article had to be photographed and preserved. We could see that the chamber had been broken into by tomb robbers probably just after burial and the intruders disturbed and left in a hurry. Various articles lay scattered on the floor as if dropped in haste, the golden legs of a throne had been broken off and lay near the throne, several jewels were found wrapped in a piece of cloth and dropped near the entrance to the second chamber. It took a long time to clear this chamber of all the treasures—but what wonderful treasures they were—the mind became blank with the sight of so many articles and the ever present glint of gold—everywhere gold. There were exquisitely painted alabaster vases, one could never hope to see equalled in beauty and a wonderful painted chest, always called afterwards as THE painted chest, inlaid with precious stone and painted in every colour one could imagine depicting scenes of battle, etc.

It was hard to imagine we were the first people to have entered the tomb for three thousand three hundred years. The thoughts WOULD come crowding into mind that the Priests who had laid Tut-Ankh-Amun to his rest had hoped that no one would ever enter the tomb as long as this world would last. Everything in the chamber held out the hope that the dead king would be reborn in an afterlife and enjoy all the things he loved on earth—and here they were. Everything in the chamber had as a reason for its presence the belief of Egypt, and as such the World, that life indeed was Eternal.

An inscription found in the tomb reads—"to speak the name of the dead is to make him live again, it restores the breath of life to the vanished."

One name lives today as no other name out of Egypt lives, the name of the Pharaoh TUT-ANKH-AMUN.

Upon leaving the tomb, the scene around took on a different aspect for a brief moment. You imagined the people of the past were still about, you pictured the burial scene of the Pharaoh, the closing of the tomb, and the events down the ages to the present day, the decline of the great Egyptian Empire, followed by the Greeks and the Romans, the Arabs and the Turks, throughout all this time the Pharaoh Tut-Ankh-Amun had slept undisturbed for over three thousand years. He was soon forgotten and following the building of the tomb of Ramesses VI, the tomb of Tut-Ankh-Amun was also forgotten, being completely hidden by the rubble and chippings caused by the excavations for the tomb above.

These thoughts however soon faded out as you recalled the splendour you had just seen. It would be impossible to visualize the actual splendour as it appeared to us who first saw these treasures in the Antechamber of the tomb by the light of a torch, for today they are laid out as so much merchandise in the Cairo Museum and the true meaning of all their glory has departed.

When the Burial Chamber was eventually opened, the first object we saw was the great gilt shrine (one of three). It was 9 feet high and as we found afterwards—17 feet long and 11 feet wide. It was overlaid with gold and almost filled the chamber, the walls were painted with brilliantly coloured scenes and inscriptions. Around the shrine resting on the ground, there were a number of funerary emblems, and at the far end, the seven magic oars the King would need to ferry himself across the waters of the underworld.

The great folding doors were closed and bolted—but not sealed. Upon opening the doors we found a second shrine and then another until the huge quartzite sarcophagus with its three gilded coffins the last of which contained the solid gold coffin with the Mummy of Tut-Ankh-Amun.

At the far end of the burial chamber, we found another entrance to yet a smaller chamber and here lay the greatest treasures of the tomb.

Facing the doorway stood the most beautiful monument one could ever hope to see, so lovely that it made one gasp with wonder and admiration. The central portion of it consisted of a large shrine-shaped chest, completely overlaid with gold and surmounted by sacred Cobras. On each side, free standing, were statues of the four Goddesses of the dead, gracious figures with outstretched protective arms, so natural and lifelike in their pose, so pitiful and compassionate the expression upon their faces that one felt it almost a sacrilege to look at them.

Two of the statues kept their gaze firmly fixed upon their charge, whilst the other two had their heads turned looking over their shoulders towards the entrance as though to watch against surprise. There was a simple grandeur about this monument that made an appeal to the imagination. It was undoubtedly the Canopic Chest, which (we found later) contained the four golden miniature coffins for the viscera. The chest inside was made from one solid piece of Alabaster.

When the sarcophagus was opened (the lid itself weighted over a ton and a quarter) the first object to be seen was the golden effigy of the Pharaoh which filled the whole of the interior and contained the other coffins, over seven feet in length. It was a wonderful sight. Upon the forehead of the Mummy mask were the emblems of the Cobra and the Vulture, also made of gold. On top of these was a wreath of flowers Howard Carter suggested were no doubt placed there by the young Queen as a farewell gift, and in his notes he writes, "Among all that regal splendour, that royal magnificence—everywhere the glint of gold, there was nothing so beautiful as those few withered flowers, still retaining their tinge of colour. They told us what a short period three thousand three hundred years really is—but Yesterday and the Morrow. In fact that little touch of nature made that ancient and our modern civilization kin."

When the mummy was revealed and the wrappings removed, one could only stand and gaze, bereft of thought, action or words.

To gaze upon the features of one who had lived those many centuries ago, to see him as a civilization long since departed had seen him, and to know that you are looking at the face of an actual Pharaoh of Egypt, who had ruled so vast an Empire long, long ago, is an experience that happens but once in a lifetime.

The face appeared to be looking back at you, eyes wide open, mockingly, what questions were being asked after all this time, and what answers were expected? Who can tell?

I left the tomb and from the Antechamber and the Burial Chamber, from that huge sarcophagus and its golden coffin came out into the modern world my thoughts still lingering over the splendour of that vanished dynasty.

* * * * * * * *

The publisher of this work wishes to confirm that those of Harry Burton's photographs that have been included in this book were licensed from the Griffith Institute, Ashmolean Museum, Oxford—now the official custodian of Howard Carter's archaeological records. Other contemporary photographs have been reproduced by permission of Times Newspapers Limited.

BIBLIOGRAPHY

The following published works were used by the author as research and reference sources for this book.

Baines, John and Malek, Jaromir. *Atlas of Ancient Egypt.* Oxford: Phaidon Press, 1958.

Carter, Howard. *The Tomb of Tutankhamen.* New York: E.P. Dutton, 1972 (originally published as *The Tomb of Tutankh-Amen* by Howard Carter and Arthur C. Mace, Volumes I-III, London, 1923, 1927, 1933).

Cheiro (Count Louis Hamon). *Real Life Stories: A Collection of Sensational Personal Experiences.* London: Herbert Jenkins Ltd., 1934.

Deeb, Marius. *Party Politics in Egypt: the Wafd & its rivals - 1919-1939.* London: Ithaca Press, 1979.

Frayling, Christopher. *The Face of Tutankhamun.* London: Faber & Faber Ltd., 1992.

Hoving, Thomas. *Tutankhamun: The Untold Story.* New York: Simon & Schuster, 1978.

Mallakh, Kamal El and Brackman, Arnold C. *The Gold of Tutankhamen.* New York: Newsweek Books, 1978.

Mansfield, Peter. *The British in Egypt.* New York: Holt, Rinehart and Winston, 1971.

Reeves, Nicholas. *The Complete Tutankhamun: The King, The Tomb, The Royal Treasure.* London: Thames and Hudson, 1990.

Winstone, H.V.F. *Howard Carter and the Discovery of the Tomb of Tutankhamun.* London: Constable & Co., 1991.

Wynne, Barry. *Behind the Mask of Tutankhamen.* Los Angeles: Pinnacle Books, 1972, and London: Souvenir Press, 1972.

* * * * * * * * *

FURTHER READING

Should the reader desire further study material regarding the life and times of Pharaoh Tutankhamun, the discovery of his tomb, or on ancient Egypt in general, the following additional reading matter is recommended by the author.

Aldred, Cyril. *The Egyptians.* London: Thames Hudson, 1984.

Aldred, Cyril. *Tutankhamun's Egypt.* London: British Broadcasting Corporation, 1972.

Andrews, Carol. *Ancient Egyptian Jewellery.* London: British Museum Publications, 1990.

Clark, Somers and Engelbach R. *Ancient Egyptian Construction and Archetecture.* New York: Dover, 1990.

Cottrell, Leonard. *The Secrets of Tutankhamen.* London: Evans Brothers, 1965.

David, Rosalie. *Cult of the Sun: Myth and Magic in Ancient Egypt.* London: J.M. Dent & Sons.

Dodson, Aidan. *Monarchs of the Nile.* London: Ribicon Press, 1995.

Edwards, I.E.S. *Tutankhamun: His Tomb and its Treasures.* New York: Metropolitan Museum of Art & Alfred A. Knopf, Inc., 1976.

Forbes, Dennis C. (ed. dir.). *KMT - A Modern Journal of Ancient Egypt.* San Francisco: KMT Communications, 1990 to date.

Hepper, F. Nigel. *Pharaoh's Flowers: The Botanical Treasures of Tutankhamun.* London: HMSO, 1990.

Rohl, David M. *A Test of Time - The Bible from Myth to History.* London: Century, 1995.

Spencer, Patricia (ed.). *Egyptian Archaeology: The Bulletin of the Egypt Exploration Society.* London: Egypt Exploration Society, 1991 to date.

Thomas, Angela P. *Akhenaten's Egypt.* Princes Risborough: Shire Publications, 1988.

Time-Life. *Egypt - Land of the Pharaohs.* Virginia: Time-Life Books (Lost Civilization Series), 1992.

Welsh, Francis. *Tutankhamun's Egypt.* Princes Risborough: Shire Publications, 1993.

* * * * * * * * *

INDEX

* * * * * * * * *